R IS FOR ROSE

R IS FOR ROSE

REFLECTIONS FROM A PASSIONATE ROSE LOVER

CAROLYN PARKER

Horticulture Books
An Imprint of F+W Publications, Inc.
Cincinnati, Ohio

09 08 07 06 05   5 4 3 2 1

Distributed in Canada by Fraser Direct
100 Armstrong Avenue
Georgetown, ON, Canada L7G 5S4
Tel: (905) 877-4411

Distributed in the U.K. and Europe by David & Charles
Brunel House, Newton Abbot, Devon, TQ12 4PU,
England
Tel: (+44) 1626 323200, Fax: (+44) 1626 323319
Email: mail@davidandcharles.co.uk

Distributed in Australia by Capricorn Link
P.O. Box 704, S. Windsor, NSW 2756 Australia
Tel: (02) 4577-3555

Library of Congress Cataloging-in-Publication Data
Parker, Carolyn
  R is for rose : reflections from a passionate rose lover /
Carolyn Parker.
       p. cm.
  Includes bibliographical references.
  ISBN 1-55870-759-X (alk. paper)
  1. Roses--Varieties. 2. Roses--Varieties--Pictorial
works. I. Title.
   SB411.6.P37 2005
   635.9'33734--dc22
                                              2005007717

Editor: Christine Doyle
Designer: Karla Baker
Production Coordinator: Robin Richie

Carolyn Parker is a New York fashion designer and stylist turned passionate gardener and floral photographer. She is the author and photographer of *The Poetry of Roses*, an illustrated anthology of rose poems. She currently works as a garden designer and floral arranging consultant while selling her photographs through Getty Images. She is also a professional speaker and member of the Garden Writers Association of America. Carolyn lives in Lafayette, California. See more roses on her Web site: www.rosesfromatoz.com.

metric conversion chart

To convert	to	multiply by
Inches	Centimeters	2.54
Centimeters	Inches	0.4
Feet	Centimeters	30.5
Centimeters	Feet	0.03
Yards	Meters	0.9
Meters	Yards	1.1
Sq. Inches	Sq. Centimeters	6.45
Sq. Centimeters	Sq. Inches	0.16
Sq. Feet	Sq. Meters	0.09
Sq. Meters	Sq. Feet	10.8
Sq. Yards	Sq. Meters	0.8
Sq. Meters	Sq. Yards	1.2
Pounds	Kilograms	0.45
Kilograms	Pounds	2.2
Ounces	Grams	28.3
Grams	Ounces	0.035

ACKNOWLEDGMENTS

When I began writing this book, I knew I needed a group of readers to keep me focused, grounded, and grammatical. Ten wonderful women entered my rose world and made themselves at home. Ronnie Deitrick, teacher and flower arranger, urged me to write more personally. Susan Donley, florist extraordinaire, cheered me, lent vases, and chauffeured in England. Mary Beale Knowles, a great garden designer, inspired and supported ideas, whims, and adventures. Writers Rachel Dacus, Susie Kohl, and Sandy Eacker kept me on track. Joeve Wilkinson, Judy Washbond, Robineve Cole, Stephanie Monson, and all the above welcomed each installment, generously gave suggestions, and relished learning more about roses.

Bob Cowden, founder of the horticultural library and the rose garden at Heather Farms, who died in 2003, went out of his way to help me with rose research. Miriam Wilkins, founder of The Heritage Roses Group, and rosarian Barbara Worl encouraged me and helped me locate Graham Stuart Thomas. Jolene Adams, horticultural judge and consulting rosarian, gave me valued suggestions in the nick of time. Gregg Lowery, Roger Phillips, Michael Marriott, Lynne Storm, Judy Dean, and Jim Delahanty kindly gave me rose tours, advice, and information.

Graham Stuart Thomas, who passed away in 2003, welcomed me into his home and poured forth from his vast store of rose experience.

Thank you and great appreciation to the poets who made translations: Rachel Dacus, Richard Deane, and Dot and Owen Cooper.

Thanks to photographers Jim MacKinnon and David Allen, the most generous friends a photographer could ask for.

Thank you Eve Fagan for 'Kathleen' and the use of your treasured vessels. Thank you Francesca Cole and Oneita Parker for posing with roses. Thank you Bonnie Forman for your cheer and for always being there when I needed manuscript assistance. Thanks Anna for making me happy. Thank you Barbara Brustman for your unique interest in my work. Thank you to all our neighbors who love the roses and our garden.

I love beautiful layouts and typography almost as much as roses. The editing and design team at F+W gave me the very best—my deepest thanks to Christine Doyle, Karla Baker, and Robin Richie. And a big bouquet of thank yous to Tricia Waddell at F+W and my agent Janet Rosen at Sheree Bykojsky Associate for believing in this project.

Thank you Leroy for your exquisite art throughout these pages. Special gratitude to Ivy, Jim, Bhau, and Carol, who inspire eternal rose presentations.

And thank you roses from *A* to *Z* for your inspiration and for allowing me, on several occasions, to photograph all of you at once!

contents

THE GIFT OF ROSES

Opposite: The lovely face of 'Just Joey' **Above:** Rose petals in a footed glass bowl

Roses offer many gifts: beauty, color, fragrance, presence, variety, diversity…. They inspire joy, internal communion, creativity, art, poetry, pastime, celebration, life change, transformation….

When I finally had the opportunity to grow roses, I found the blooms, no matter how small, gave me more than I gave them. Each new discovery seemed profound and miraculous. While gardening, an internal dialogue opened that prompted wishes to share my story and the wonder of roses.

In 1984, my family—husband Leroy and our two daughters, Oneita and Anna—moved into our home on an expansive corner lot in Lafayette, California. The garden consisted of a weedy lawn bordered by a two-foot-high split rail fence, an assortment of neglected evergreen shrubs, six towering trees, two sprinkler attachments, and three rosebushes.

I had not gardened since 1976; my career as a fashion designer kept me working at a cutting table in my studio. Silk and velvet were my fertile soil. Fabric cutouts appliquéd on luxurious evening wear took the place of butterflies and flowers. The only roses in sight were on calendar photos pinned to the bulletin board. Little did I know back then that our third of an acre in suburbia would be the perfect focus of unlimited possibilities with roses.

After ten years of squeezing gardening time into sixty-hour workweeks and annual selling trips to New York, my business partner and I felt a sudden urge for change. Quite unexpectedly, we closed our design studio. I had no plans for the future but stepped passionately into the role of gardener. I soon felt I was playing a part in an unknown and greater plan.

Our first plantings, along the fence in front of the house, were twelve rose-bushes my husband propagated from previous gardens. The roses thrived. As we removed old junipers and continued to transform our property, friends and neighbors offered us more rosebushes. One autumn, I impulsively purchased eight white rosebushes. In our third winter, I ordered thirty bare root roses from a catalog, sight unseen! We chopped down two huge ash trees so the roses would not be robbed of moisture. I bought books on roses and wore them out leafing through beautiful pictures.

The substance and beauty of roses resonated deep within me. Watching a newly planted rose bloom for the first time inspired me to grow roses in abundance. Without a formal plan, roses became our garden's theme and my life's delight. I spent my days quietly observing, learning about, and working in the garden with nature as my new partner. In the front garden, open to public view, we expanded flower beds with more roses, perennials, and flowering shrubs. In the secluded back garden, I created a shade garden, formal herb beds, and cutting and vegetable gardens.

As the garden progressed, with its intoxicating beauty, I tried capturing the magic on film. I started a small flower business specializing in baskets of roses, which I also recorded with my camera. I sold greeting cards made from many of the photographs. All the while, my rose fervor surprised me. I couldn't help feeling I would one day have my work more widely published.

My photographs improved, and I decided to take a portfolio to New York to show publishers. I presented my photography the way my partner and I used to show buyers a fashion collection. *The Poetry of Roses*, my first book, was the result. The pleasure of choosing rose poems for the book and illustrating them with my photographs brought me even closer to roses.

One day, in early spring 1999, while enjoying the first blooms on climbing 'Rouletii', an idea came to me: *make an* R *out of 'Rouletii' as the capi-*

Carolyn standing under the arch of 'Rouletii'

tal letter for the word Rose. Being a fan of decorative typography, I thought I could photograph and scan the *R* to use with computer fonts. I carefully shaped the tiny pink roses, branches, and leaves into the letter. The finished design brought out the distinct charm of 'Rouletii's' personality. Intrigued when I realized that 'Rouletii' also formed its own initial, I gathered branches of Banks roses to form the letter *B*. I was soon compelled to create an entire alphabet in roses and began to plan representatives of *A* through *Z*.

My favorite roses took up alphabet letters first: Foetida Bicolor, 'Moss', and 'Sweet Surrender'. Then royal members in the history of genus *Rosa* gave *A*, *B*, and *X* their places. The roses 'Graham Thomas', 'Iceberg', and 'Just Joey' won spots for their vigor and beauty. I had to choose from several candidates for *D* and *W*; 'Duet' edged out 'Double Delight'; 'White Masterpiece' overcame 'William Baffin'. When the list was complete, to my amazement, our garden contained all but four of the alphabet's roses. *K*, *N*, *V*, and *Z* were the most difficult spots to fill. Few rose names begin with those letters. I had to wait a year to acquire 'Zéphirine Drouhin'.

Choosing the roses, at first, seemed like a chance meeting of twenty-six rosebushes, but then it became obvious that each rose was a celebrity and had a compelling story to tell. The rose alphabet blossomed into this book! By focusing on only twenty-six roses, I can show, through my photographs, how the individual roses grow and how they love to be harvested and arranged. And the

'Buff Beauty' underplanted with catmint, cream California poppies, and fleabane against the fence at our side garden.

rose alphabet created the perfect format to share the wealth of information my love for roses has given me.

These roses form a diverse group: Species, singles, sports, antiques, climbers, Hybrid Teas, and English Roses are just some that are represented. After writing the first few chapters, it seemed to me that the roses had been carefully chosen long ago, and I was simply their scribe. Each rose imparts a unique store of knowledge that uncannily paves the way for the next rose.

My research revealed how the earth has become a rich repository of the genus *Rosa*. The roses introduce remarkable people responsible for this flourishing lineage. The early chapters created a historical framework that eventually encouraged passages of deep personal reflection.

Many of the chapters refer to England's pivotal role in the rose world. I wrote

Queen Anne's lace and nigella surround 'Perfume Delight'.

from photographic and textual references along with my own rich imaginings. Then one day, one of my manuscript readers, moved by the chapter on England's beloved rosarian Graham Stuart Thomas, asked if I had ever been to England. After I said no, she wished I would go, to meet Graham and to see the famous places I write about.

I mentioned this to my friend Susan Donley who is a rose gardener and florist. Since she loves roses as much as I do and happens to have a brother living in London, the idea became a reality when, two months later, we toured gardens at the peak of England's rose bloom. Many chapters have been enriched by our English rose adventures.

Each rose is unique, and her personality shines in a container. In the arranging section, you'll find valuable information on how to construct bouquets like the ones on these pages.

Throughout the book, I speak of roses with female pronouns unless, of course, they are named after a man. I can't call blooms of such gorgeous femininity *it*. Also, I mention roses blooming in the spring, because in California roses begin to bloom in March.

Twenty years after planting the first roses in our garden, a lattice deer fence has replaced the split rail fence. We have more than 150 rosebushes planted in eight-foot-wide beds inside the fence. At least a hundred more roses grow in other places throughout the garden. I still have those two sprinklers, and two of the original rosebushes (names unknown) continue to supply their bounty of yellow and pink blossoms.

Please join my roses and me as we weave a wreath of bounty and generosity with fresh, new ways of living with and loving roses.

I hope you like your initials,
CP

Hand-tied posies of alphabet members dress up mayonnaise jars.

ALBA, ROSA RUGOSA

'Alba' clusters float in a shallow bowl.

"What kind of plant is that?" asked a neighbor, as we admired spring growth on the roses.

I answered, "*Rosa rugosa alba*."

Looking at the dull, spindly branches, he replied, "That's a rosebush? It looks prehistoric!"

Since *Rosa rugosa alba* is one of my favorites, I came to her defense. "This shrub will soon be a gorgeous, leafy mound any gardener would be honored to grow."

Later I realized my neighbor had intuited the truth. Rugosa roses are among the most ancient species roses in existence. Centuries before gardeners made note of them, they flourished wild along the sandy beaches of Siberia, China, and Japan. The Japanese first mentioned the species in the twelfth century. They produced a perfume with petals of this rose mixed with camphor and musk.

Rugosas reached European shores in 1796. New York nurseryman Thomas Hogg introduced the Japanese form to the United Sates in 1872. The shrubs have since naturalized on both coasts and are sometimes referred to as "coast roses." I've seen pictures of dense thickets thriving at Martha's Vineyard on the Atlantic coast,

FAINTLY FRAGRANT, THE AIR AROUND AN 'RUGOSA ALBA' BLOOM SOFTENS WITH REFRESHMENT.

and I've enjoyed Rugosas in beach towns along the Pacific coast in Oregon.

I saw my first 'Rugosa Alba' in the Berkeley Rose Garden in the late sixties. My husband and I always visited the Rugosa beds near the tennis courts to marvel at their beauty. They displayed a fascinating combination of glossy, deeply veined foliage, pure white, tissue-thin flower petals, and bulbous green, orange, and red hips. Of all the roses in the Berkeley garden, I wanted to grow this one.

Planted eighteen years ago, our 'Rugosa Alba' often stops pedestrians who

'Schneezwerg's' hips, like patent leather

'Rugosa Alba' is laden with hips in late autumn 2004.

pass by. People think the large, ripe hips are juicy cherry tomatoes. Startled, they look again when they realize tomatoes don't grow with fluttery, five-petal flowers measuring four inches across! The open blooms, filled with cavorting bumblebees whose legs are laden with pollen, fascinate the neighborhood children.

The word *alba* in a plant name indicates that the flowers are white. And to avoid rose-world confusion, Alba also names a small class of fragrant, hardy, white and pale pink Old Roses, descended from a natural cross of a Species rose with a Damask.

Faintly fragrant, the air around an 'Rugosa Alba' bloom softens with refreshment. I sometimes snack on the meaty, vitamin C-rich hips while working in the garden. Under the tangy soft skin,

'Rugosa Alba' in spring 2005, before the hips turned orange

fleshy, sweet-tasting fiber encases sturdy seeds. Not all the hips mature into fruit; some bunches dry up. Deadheading Rugosas is unnecessary. If you don't mind snipping off blemished hips and if you can ignore the sight of the awkward canes during winter dormancy, you will be rewarded with a carefree, exceptionally disease-resistant rosebush.

Another Rugosa benefit worth mentioning is that deer don't eat them. They may nip a few of the first buds of spring but after that, they leave my shrubs alone.

Rosa rugosa alba has an equally ancient magen-

ta twin called *Rosa rugosa*. Her vivid coloring makes me wonder if she was the first flower to express magenta. Someone once told me that magenta symbolizes true love.

There are also a number of Rugosa hybrids; one I especially like is 'Schneezwerg'. Her ruffled white blooms set small hips that shine like red patent leather.

During travels to other habitats, I enjoy looking for familiar plants to see how they might differ. En route to London from Heathrow Airport, I was excited to see white and magenta Rugosas and small, wild roses (*R. canina*) competing for growing space in the tightly packed weeds, grasses, and shrubbery of hedgerows

Above: Three Rugosa branches form an opulent base for long-stemmed roses and Japanese anemones inserted in a large ceramic vase made by my husband, Leroy Parker. **Opposite:** The magenta *Rosa rugosa*

along the motorway. On our first day of garden touring, I saw 'Alba' in Vita Sackville-West's rose garden at Sissinghurst Castle. I was surprised that they were six-foot mounds. Since I prune mine back halfway each winter, in my hot California garden, our shrub only reaches three or four feet. Nearly every English garden we visited had massive shrubs of both Rugosas. They must adore the moist climate, because they were sometimes ten feet high!

Rugosas naturalized on beaches in the United States are kept closer to the ground by the wind, and their suckers spread into extensive drifts. I wondered why my shrub didn't sucker. Later, I realized it never would because it is budded to foreign rootstock. I recently purchased Rugosas in each color on their own roots. They have eager suckers that have already emerged through the dirt ready to establish new growth.

In the garden, Rugosas and their decorative hips are a wonderful focal point. They make useful hedges, rustic barrier plantings, and showy backgrounds for perennial gardens. Since Rugosas originally stabilized sandy dunes, they are also good for erosion control. Rugosas are not particular about soil and can withstand extreme cold and strong winds. From May to October, our shrub is rarely without blooms. Few rosebushes can boast such a record. In the fall her leaves turn a rich gold.

The primal nature of *Rosa rugosa alba* and her enduring presence on earth, make her the perfect rose to begin this alphabet.

banksia lutea

BANKSIA LUTEA

'Lady Banks' introduced herself to me with long, arching canes of butter yellow flowers that reached over the fence from our neighbor's side garden. Masses of tiny, pom-pom-like flowers with tiny green centers and thornless branches gave me no clue that she was a rose. Her leaves were flimsy and thin, but when I noticed the leafstalks had an odd number of leaflets arranged in pairs with a leader at the tip, I knew. All roses share this leaf structure—a handy identifier if you come across an unfamiliar shrub.

As soon as I became acquainted with our neighbor's new planting, I spotted 'Lady Banks' scrambling forty feet up a tree in a nearby backyard and growing in mounds, as big as a house, on the side of a freeway. While traveling in Assisi, Italy, I identified an avalanche of her pale blooms cascading from a steeply terraced garden.

The capabilities of 'Lady Banks' astonish me. She is one of the most vigorous of all

This ceramic vase with a wisteria design (made by my husband, Leroy) inspired me to gather a big bucket of fully open Banksia branches. I lifted out the entire bunch with both hands and inserted the stems into the vase for a lavish arrangement-free presentation.

roses. With one long, magnificent bloom span, 'Lady Banks' heralds spring as one of the first roses to bloom in our garden.

There are four forms of *Rosa banksiae*: two singles (five petals per bloom) and two doubles (more than twenty-one petals per bloom). They come from China where they flourish along roadsides and edge planted fields. From 1796 to 1824,

WITH ONE LONG, MAGNIFICENT BLOOM SPAN,
'LADY BANKS' HERALDS SPRING AS ONE OF
THE FIRST ROSES TO BLOOM IN OUR GARDEN.

plant collectors sailing the globe for unusual specimens brought three of the four roses to England. William Kerr discovered the double white form growing in Canton in 1807 and named it 'Lady Banks'. The name honored the wife of his benefactor, Sir Joseph Banks, who funded the Royal Botanic Gardens at Kew in London.

A Banksia leaf next to a regular rose leaf illustrates their differences.

Banks became the *banksiae* class: *normalis* is the white single and *lutescens* is the yellow single. *Alba plena*, the double white, has a fragrance of sweet violets. I'd tried numerous times to detect scent on our yellow *luteas* and had found none, not even a hint, though I've read to the contrary in several places. Until the autumn of 2001, I thought Banksia Lutea was the only nonfragrant rose in my alphabet.

Scent is a sensitive and highly personal subject with roses. At some rose shows, judges use an eight-category grading range from "scent just detectable" to "supremely scented." Many people won't even buy a rose if it isn't fragrant. When a rose has little fragrance I sometimes like it all the more. The subtle waft of scent seems so pure. On the first of November, while training long Banksia canes, I saw a sprig of blooms among masses of canes. How odd, I thought, she only blooms in the spring. A quirk of fate gave me a second chance to check for fragrance. I plucked the tiny cluster and held it to my nose. It was fragrant! The rose that I said had no fragrance smelled fresh, violetlike, and very pleasant. The perfume didn't last long, but it was there. You never know when a rose will release her aroma.

Single Banks roses are rare and considered the true species. In London, we visited Roger Phillips, who describes seeing Banks roses growing in China in his book, co-authored with Martyn Rix, *The Quest for the Rose*. To my astonishment, he pointed to a towering *normalis* growing up a tree in his garden at Eccleston Square. I had dreamed of growing this white single. He gave me several cuttings to

Banksia Lutea grows along the fence on our property line.

root and told me he planted his rose from seed he obtained in China!

The two double varieties, said to be sports, are readily available in nurseries. Since a number of roses in my alphabet are sports, I'd like to give a clear definition of this fascinating occurrence in the plant world. A *sport* is a growth that mutates on an existing shrub with a different color or growth habit. In the case of 'Lady Banks', a shrub bearing single flowers sported new branches with double

flowers. These new flowering branches were then propagated into shrubs of double flowers.

Give 'Lady Banks' plenty of space if you have it, and let her grow naturally. In Tombstone, Arizona, a white Banks planted in 1884 now covers 8,000 square feet on an arbor that shelters 150 seats!

If you have a large property, unpruned Banks roses can be very effective blooming in the spring landscape. Banks roses grow easily from cuttings and require no watering once established. Our shrubs have never been fertilized. However, they are tender and cannot consistently survive winters below United States Department of Agriculture (USDA) Zone 9.

If you don't mind pruning, Banks roses can be tamed. Our bushes are usually pruned as a manageable hedge since they grow along a narrow walkway. Once, I trained a cane to weave down the length of the fence—growth stopped when I clipped it at the last post after traveling eighteen feet!

Before China's "repeat-blooming" roses entered the gene pool, most roses in the West bloomed only once. Banks roses bloom once on wood from the previous year. Other once-bloomers like 'Common Moss' (page 94) bloom on the current season's growth. The rose gardener plans pruning strategy according to these individual blooming traits.

While blooming, 'Lady Banks' sends out new canes that won't bloom until the next spring. In our garden, this growth often has mildew. We chop it off after the bloom. Another set of fresh-leafed canes will appear before long.

As spring approaches, you have the choice of leaving the canes long or cutting them short. Both ways, they will fill with bloom. On the long canes, every leaf juncture will sprout one or more bloom clusters.

You don't have to be particular about where you make your pruning cuts on a Banks rose; but I found that you can prune the bushes too late in the season. One year, gardeners pruned ours in late winter just before the flower buds were about to set. Sadly, we had no blooms that year.

If you like to arrange roses, plan your entertaining schedule around springtime's once-

A handblown glass bud vase highlights one small sprig.

bloomers. 'Lady Banks' is magnificent in an interior setting. Take a good look at the long canes and notice how they begin blooming close to the bush. In a season of mild weather, the little flowers can take up to a month to bloom all the way out to the cane's tip. Amazingly, the first roses to bloom are still fresh when the tip roses finally open. In big arrangements, they are especially stunning when all the blooms are open. At all stages, you can have fun picking little clusters to display in small vases. The round, unopened buds are especially appealing.

It has been a pleasure to become acquainted with 'Lady Banks' and share her winning qualities with you. Thanks to our neighbor, my rose alphabet has a marvelous *B*.

Two Banksia canes inserted in water vials decorate the handle on a basket of strawberries.

CÉCILE BRÜNNER

‘Cécile Brünner’ stars in a table centerpiece while sprigs of her pink flowers peek out of matching napkins.

"'Climbing Cécile Brünner'—four rosebushes for the price of three!" The tantalizing catalog offer prompted my sister Judy to place an order. I asked her if she knew that these climbers grow to mammoth proportions and are capable of knocking down the structures they're tied to. She had no idea; in her vision, delicate roses climbed up the walls of her house and over arches. Judy's plans changed after I told her my 'Cécile' saga.

Like my sister, I thought the ideal rose garden should include what has become known as the "sweetheart rose" for her miniature, perfectly shaped buds. Popular for decades, old neighborhoods near us have a 'Cécile Brünner' in almost every garden. I planned to feature her climbing over an arch to create a romantic passage from our shade garden to the sunny herb beds. I ordered two of the climbers and a metal arch from a garden catalog.

The newly planted 'Cécile Brünner' roses were two feet high in the spring of 1990.

A year later, they had reached the top of the arch. I was as proud of their achievement as if it were my own. By 1992, leafy canes covered with roses hid the arch in a glorious display. The next year, the rose arch became my photo muse. Two

A YEAR LATER, THE 'CÉCILE BRÜNNER' ROSES HAD REACHED THE TOP OF THE ARCH. I WAS AS PROUD OF THEIR ACHIEVEMENT AS IF IT WERE MY OWN.

striking pictures from this time appear in my book, *The Poetry of Roses*. Maybe the pictures inspired my sister's vision.

In a beribboned vase, 'Cécile' blooms make a dear gift.

By the fifth year, the bushes were so vigorous I wondered if the arch would continue to hold them. We finally had to prop the arch up with two-by-fours. In year seven, the whole thing toppled over and dainty 'Cécile' looked like a beached whale crushing our herb beds.

We hoisted the metal arch back up with a long wire attached to an enormous silver maple to await a sturdy pergola. 'Climbing Cécile Brünner' needs a hefty garden structure built with nothing smaller than four-by-fours.

'Cécile Brünner' has sharp thorns and is extremely vigorous. Unless you have unlimited space where the twenty-foot climber can grow wild, or you have an old building you want to camouflage, this rose requires no-nonsense pruning by a strong person wearing sturdy leather gloves, who can work on a ladder and make cut after cut with arms raised.

If your 'Cécile Brunner' is a nice, civilized shrub, you might think I am overdramatizing the growth habits of 'Climbing Cécile Brünner'. We also have such a shrub, and it has been growing in our gardens for twenty-seven years with little pruning. How can the same two roses have such different growth habits?

Produced by the Ducher nursery in France, this rose, classified as Polyantha, has disputed parentage. She was named 'Mlle Cécile Brünner' after the daughter of renowned Swiss nurseryman Ulrich Brünner and introduced to commerce in 1881. A rose lover touring France purchased one of the special new shrubs and brought it all the way to

California to plant in her garden. One day, she noticed a cane growing eight feet longer than all of the others! The energetic sport was cut off and propagated to create new rosebushes that retained the same vigorous growth pattern. The cloned versions were called 'Climbing Cécile Brünner' and debuted in 1894.

After the grand spring bloom, a few roses appear now and then throughout the summer. Several years ago, Heirloom Roses, a rose mail-

My *Poetry of Roses* photo muse

order company in Oregon, put out the word that they were looking for a 'Climbing Cécile Brünner' sport with a strong repeat bloom. They received one and now offer the improved version in their catalog.

'Mlle Cécile Brünner' also sported a pillar rose called 'Spray Cécile Brünner', which grows four times as large as the original and blooms in great clusters along lax canes that soar against the skylight. If you love 'Cécile' but have a small space, Ralph Moore of Sequoia Nursery hybridized a mini version that is a healthy twelve-inch plant.

On our climber, vigorous new cane growth follows the bloom. We either shear this growth off as flat as a boxwood hedge or leave it long and luxurious. Our two climbers are disease-free. Sometimes they have a little black spot, but mildew does not affect them and aphids don't attack the buds.

A bench at the back of our herb garden faces the 'Cécile Brünner' arch. During her bloom, I love to invite my husband or friends to sit with me to share a front row seat on pure dazzle. 'Climbing Cécile Brünner's' deep green foliage is also beautiful without blooms—our garden and my alphabet would feel incomplete without her presence.

To illustrate how 'Cécile Brünner' provides all things to the flower arranger, one photo shows three arrangements. The medium arrangement is hand-gathered, while the sizeable branches in the large vase were inserted. (See Arranging Roses, page 188.)

DUET

'Duet' joined our garden eighteen years ago as one of the roses in my first bare root catalog order. A photograph showing her wavy petals of silvery pink backed with rose crimson placed her at the top of my wish list.

Bare root means the plants are winter-dormant and sold without soil. I'll never forget opening the box. It came on an overcast, winter afternoon and contained a mass of moist, prickled canes and wispy roots tied together and tagged with three fanciful names. The plants appeared fragile and mysterious. Instructions inside the box informed me how to care for them. I couldn't wait to plant the bare skeletons and watch them fulfill their internal code.

Dependable, disease-resistant 'Duet' outlasted the other roses in that initial order. All these years, she has remained a shapely three-by-four-foot shrub while producing armloads of fragrant blooms. The two-toned flowers glow in the garden, producing both clusters and single-stemmed roses.

Compared to the first three roses in my alphabet, 'Duet' is a newcomer whose growth structure is more typical of modern roses. She is a Hybrid Tea parented by

A PHOTOGRAPH SHOWING HER WAVY PETALS OF SILVERY PINK BACKED WITH ROSE CRIMSON PLACED HER AT THE TOP OF MY WISH LIST.

'Fandango' and 'Rondelay', raised by Herbert Swim, and introduced to the world in 1960.

'Duet's' quick rebloom, and even her name, encourages both garden appreciation and experimentation with arranging. Many gardeners are so in love with how a blooming rosebush looks they wouldn't dare harvest the display. I like to know how a rosebush behaves in the garden and how its blooms look in a vase.

Bare root roses ready to be planted

Without a second thought, I'll cut every blooming stem for an arrangement.

Even though I harvested all of 'Duet's' mature blooms for the pictures shown here, several days later there was another flush. The roses finished blooming on July 24. The first roses in new clusters began blooming on August 15! Not all Hybrid Teas are this productive, but good planting and fertilizing techniques are a big help.

Choosing a rose that is adaptable to your climate is your most important consideration and requires some investigation. In San Francisco, many-petaled roses don't do well because they don't receive enough sun; in Maine gardens, the winters are so severe most roses are treated as annuals. The Vintage Gardens catalog (see Resources, page 204), which lists over 2,600 roses, provides information on roses for specific climates.

The Vintage catalog also has excellent illustrations to signify growth habit and size, your next most important considerations. You'll be way ahead

Fresh 'Duet' petals make a dramatic short-term arrangement.

if you research the mature sizes of the roses you want to plant before you order them. I have made many planting mistakes, especially with impulse purchases. Delectable small, young rosebushes sometimes end up in tight spots, and two years later I'm surprised when they have become huge shrubs.

In the garden, roses love a nice sunny location that is free of invading roots from other plants or trees. They prefer a minimum of six hours of sun, and they especially like morning sun. Rich, well-

A   The freshly harvested bucket of 'Duet' blooms.

B   The slim metal vase cinches in the stems for the easiest containment.

C   A ceramic pot by Leroy Parker contains blooms similar to the bucket.

D   The broad volume of the square vase requires more adjusting to keep the stems from spreading.

E   The narrow neck and base of the ginger jar also contain the stems, like the bucket.

F   The bunch is divided and hand-tied.

Sometimes leaving the stems in the bucket isn't appropriate for an arrangement. Here I chose five vases with an eye to how they are similar to the bucket's volume. The ceramic pot, ginger jar, and metal vase were easy and required no arranging. The square vase and the two smaller vases needed a little arranging to achieve a pretty presentation.

drained soil is a must for healthy roses. The addition of organic material enriches and binds sandy soil, and clay soil (like mine) breaks down and lightens as it is enhanced.

Color coordination might also be important to you. My roses get moved at the whim of my ever-changing ideas about color harmony. My garden has gone from a multicolored panorama to a story of graduated color change. 'Duet' is in her original spot, but all the roses around her are now in the same warm tones.

As a gardener, I have a sentimental bond with 'Duet' as my first mail-order rose, but it's her continuous bloom, graceful form, and longevity that earn her a well-deserved spot in my rose alphabet.

'Duet' hand-gathered with candy stripe sweet peas

Single stems adorn bud vases.

PLANTING BARE ROOT ROSES

Be prepared to give your newly arrived bare root roses immediate care. Place the roots in water overnight for a long drink, but note that leaving the roots in water longer than twenty-four hours will decrease a rose's vigor when planted. If you need to wait up to a week to plant, heel-in the canes (that is to say, bury the roots) in compost. Another alternative is to plant the rose temporarily in a five-gallon pot. However, you'll need to wait to transplant the rose until after the first bloom when the root-ball is mature enough to stay intact while dislodging the plant from the pot. If you opt to plant your rose in a compressed paper pot, the pot can go directly into a planting hole.

Pick the first short-stemmed blooms from a cluster for display in votives or small vases.

ELINA

'Philadelphus' branches in an enamel pitcher support the easy insertion of one 'Elina' rose at a time.

My heart leaped the first time I saw the buds of 'Elina'. As I eased my way through a rose-crowded aisle in the San Francisco Flower Mart, my eyes thrilled at the sight of her swirling centers on creamy, fat buds. I had never seen a more beautiful petal formation. I searched for the nametag on the florist bundles of cut roses, and thank goodness there was one…it said 'Peaudouce'. I had to find her for my garden.

As I began searching, I learned her name had changed to 'Elina' for the American retail market. Apparently, 'Peaudouce', French for "soft skin," conflicted with a brand name of disposable diapers! Over the next three years, my husband and I tried to find a source for this exquisite rose and finally tracked her down at the Petaluma Rose Company. Hidden away on an old country road, we found row after row of potted roses in bud. At least twenty 'Elinas' were lined up in the *E* section. Ecstatic to be in her presence again, I chose three well-caned shrubs in five-gallon cans.

'Elina', a Hybrid Tea introduced in Northern Ireland by P. Dickson in 1983, is now readily available. The upright, rather stiff, disease-resistant five-foot shrub, like most Hybrid Teas, is not known for its gracefulness in the garden. It is, how-

ONE MORNING, WITH MY EQUIPMENT READY TO ZOOM IN ON A PROMISING BUD, I SET MY EYE ON THE LENS VIEWER TO FIND A GREAT SURPRISE. THE UNFURLING CENTER PETALS HAD FORMED A TINY, PERFECT HEART!

ever, a flower arranger's dream. 'Elina' produces twenty-five to forty straight, strong stems with sturdy, one-to-a-stem blooms. The ivory buds deepen to pale yellow as they open and return to ivory as they mature. The faintly perfumed open roses last for days in a bouquet.

A large arrangement with a more complex base of greens highlights 'Elina' blooms.

'Elina' has one fault. Excessive hot or cold weather causes dark blemishes that appear on the bud's petal edges. Sometimes as the rose continues to open, the spots become less noticeable; other times they're unsightly. I find it poignant that petals of such porcelain-like perfection can be so disfigured. Being patient and hopeful is a must if you grow 'Elina'.

Hybrid Teas appear nine times in my alphabet. Each example, except for cluster-blooming 'Duet' (page 32), possesses compelling appeal as an individual bloom. Because of the continuing allure of Hybrid Teas and 'Elina's' unique charm, I want to give a brief account of the Hybrid Tea's heritage.

Less than ten species of wild roses from approximately two hundred that existed on the earth for thousands, perhaps millions, of years created ten important rose families: Gallicas, Damasks, Albas, Centifolias, Mosses, Chinas, Portlands, Bourbons, Hybrid Perpetuals, and Teas. The first five families are once-bloomers that resulted from pollen-crossings and mutations that naturally occurred when people, long before the ancient Greeks, uprooted roses from the wild and planted them together in gardens.

GROWING HYBRID TEAS

Most Hybrid Teas won't last in the garden below Zone 6B unless they are given winter protection. For protection, mounding dirt over the crown is a common practice. My sister, who lives in Zone 5, mounds leaves from her maple tree.

The next five families were sired by chance crossings of the preceding groups with the very fertile, reblooming roses imported from China in the mid-eighteenth century. Simple, loose flowers on open, airy shrubs characterize the China hybrids. They had little fragrance, but the roses rebloomed through the summer and fall. The Chinas passed on this valuable trait and paved the way for the creation of reblooming modern roses.

In the seventeenth century, man began to

assist nature when the Centifolias became popular. Hybridists gathered rose seeds at random, planted them, and made selections from the resulting seedlings. During the heyday of the Hybrid Perpetuals and Teas, the process was refined somewhat. Breeders planted roses they wanted to mate in the same bed, hoping proximity would achieve fertilization! By 1848 breeding knowledge had changed from chance to purpose. Hybridists learned to dust pollen from one parent onto the stigma of another.

The China roses had endowed the Hybrid Perpetuals and Teas with espe-

Three days after photographing the bouquet on page 40, I shot the flowers again with a light background and a different wrap. The blooms are still fresh and are now fully open!

cially desirable characteristics. With the new and experimental methods, breeders now aimed to combine the two and began hybridizing the early Hybrid Teas. In 1867, Guillot marketed 'La France', a lovely light pink rose, as the "first" Hybrid Tea. In this new rose, the genes of the Tea rose contributed an elegant, pointed, oval bud that dramatically unfurled its long petals into the Hybrid Perpetual's endowment—vigorous growth and a robust, large bloom. These traits, coupled with the reblooming habits of the Tea, made exciting new roses on a sturdy, repeat-blooming shrub. Unluckily for Monsieur Guillot, 'La France' proved to be sterile and could not be used for further hybridizing.

Fifteen years later, an English cattle breeder named Henry Bennet produced a very fertile Hybrid Tea named 'Lady Mary Fitzwilliam'. Her chromosomal bundle allowed for hearty cross-pollination within the group and within other rose groups. The ancestry of 1,300 roses can be traced back to 'Lady Mary'.

The Hybrid Tea's influence changed the rose world significantly. The next century produced tens of thousands of Hybrid Teas and numerous other new groups. At this point, there are fifty-one rose families. As our new century begins, the fervent love for roses and the quest for new forms show no signs of slowing down.

Why is the Hybrid Tea so popular? Every bloom issues an invitation to join a process of unfolding that enriches life and touches the soul. In the garden or in the protection of an interior setting, people are attracted and refreshed by the unfurling tale a Hybrid Tea has to tell. The high-centered blooms offer unconditional beauty. Twentieth century poet Rainer Maria Rilke offered his impression of this process in the first poem of his cycle, "Les Roses":

> *If your dawn-smile astonishes*
> *us, happy rose,*
> *it's that within your petals*
> *you are in deep repose.*

> *You seem wide awake,*
> *but inside sleeps ageless bliss:*
> *a silent caress that makes*
> *your heart an utmost kiss.*

TRANSLATED BY RACHEL DACUS

As a photographer, I longed to reveal the secret held within the heart of a rose's center. I kept a watchful eye on 'Elina' for good close-up opportunities. One morning, with my equipment ready to zoom in on a promising bud, I set my eye on the lens viewer to find a great surprise. The unfurling center petals had formed

The 'Elina' stems were inserted one at a time, requiring careful balancing by the arranger and cooperation from the rose.

a tiny, perfect heart! I had not seen the heart with my naked eye. I was beside myself as I clicked the shutter. The resulting photograph of the heart-shape keyhole seems to promise to reveal the secret of the rose. Since that first meeting with 'Elina' eight years ago, my heart warms every time I see her. It gives me great pleasure to introduce her in the form of an *E*.

Above: Variegated buckthorn branches were inserted in a frog to form a long low base for the roses, making this arrangement suitable for a dining table. The branches stay horizontal thanks to the frog. (See Arranging Roses, page 201.) **Opposite:** A close-up of 'Elina' and her heart-shape center

foetida bicolor

The branches in this brass urn are filled with blooms that opened the previous day; their dropping petals decorate the tray.

FOETIDA BICOLOR

One day, preoccupied with my thoughts, I drove into a parking lot behind a dull, two-story office building. As I eased my car into a space facing a rickety wooden fence, I looked up and saw flames. Wild roses blazed in deep orange-red, with gold undersides and brilliant jeweled centers. The dazzling display ascended from leafy branches that traveled along the top of the fence. Dumbstruck, I stared at this marvel. What rose could it be?

By then, wild roses had established a relationship with me; in fact I was in love with them. My special amours were the pale pink and white species roses from the fields and forests of Oregon and California. In contrast, the breed before me spoke of distant lands and of passion beyond compare.

Back at home, I remembered a book of rose paintings a friend had given me many years ago. I took the book off the shelf, and there on the cover was the fiery rose I had just seen!

The text said *Rosa foetida bicolor* came from Persia with a history that is seven-hundred years old.

I thought of the popular Persian Sufi poet Hafiz, who used the rose as a symbol of his true beloved—God. In the 1300s Hafiz wrote:

If you find yourself
in the company of the rose,
it is your precious friend.
Enjoy it to the fullest
while it is with you.

EXCERPT TRANSLATED BY DOT AND OWEN COOPER

Five years after the parking lot encounter, we planted Foetida Bicolor in a secluded area of the garden. I wanted this rose for myself. Since she blooms only once each spring, I anticipate her company each year. Excited when the flower buds finally form, I look at them every day, waiting to see the gold, tightly furled petals emerge from enclosing sepals. When the first rose opens, I gaze in awe and celebration.

EXCITED WHEN THE FLOWER BUDS FINALLY FORM, I LOOK AT THEM EVERY DAY, WAITING TO SEE THE GOLD, TIGHTLY FURLED PETALS EMERGE FROM ENCLOSING SEPALS.

How did such a rose come to be? During the springtime, in a Persian garden, a tall, slender shrub bloomed with bright yellow roses. With a beauty that was cherished throughout the land, her flower's five heart-shape petals perfectly matched their center pistils and stamens.

On a cold winter day, when the rose had no leaves, a new growth bud surfaced through an eye on one of her brown, prickly canes. As the days warmed, the pointed bud swelled, turned red, and began to lengthen. Lateral branches emerged followed by shaggy bits of green that became small, sharply serrated leaflets. When fully leafed-out, flower buds appeared.

Rosa foetida, the shrub that sported *Rosa foetida bicolor*

This occurred every year. But on this one new cane, when the sepals curled back on the rose-buds—instead of yellow—tight scrolls of gold emerged with a hint of red. Five petals slowly unfolded and took shape. The unexpected gold became the under-lining for cups of glowing crimson. At the center, the pistils formed a heart of garnet encircled by stamens of gold.

Arching out in the sun, the laden cane of two-toned, flaming blooms silently introduced a new rose to creation. The next morning, when her petals fell, her remaining circlets of golden stamens stayed bright for another day.

An astonished gardener noticed the brilliant flowers and eagerly propagated another rosebush from the sporting cane. When the new rose bloomed, all her flowers were the identical gold and crimson. She was called *Doufrouyeh* (two faces). Progeny of the pure yellow and the two-toned rose-bushes grew in cultivation from Asia Minor to Afghanistan and Eastern Tibet.

When she reached Europe, an unsympathetic fellow named the roses *R. foetida* and *R. foetida bicolor*. In Latin, *foetida* means "having a bad smell." It seems unjust to name such stunning roses for their scent. Their fragrance is unusual, more pungent than bad.

Since there were so few yellow roses and they only bloomed once, hybridists tried using the two Foetidas and another relative, Foetida 'Persiana', to make a yellow Hybrid Tea. For twenty years, the persistent Frenchman Pernet-Ducher tried without success. Then one day, a visitor in his rose fields pointed out a yellow seedling that must have come from an accidental cross. The plant turned out to possess the genes of a reblooming hybrid. Unknowingly, Pernet-Ducher finally succeeded in creating what is classified as the first yellow Hybrid Tea. He introduced her in 1900 with the name 'Soleil d'Or', meaning "golden sun."

The successful mating of 'Soleil d'Or' brought yellow to the usable gene pool. Now rose breeders have free reign for unlimited color possibilities. Thanks to the Foetidas, the world has yellow, gold, peach, orange, coral, and multicolored roses. Many of these roses' lack of fragrance can be traced to the Foetidas, and they are also blamed for introducing black spot to roses.

The Foetida Bicolor shrub grows to a height of five or six feet. After the first flush of blooms, new leaves emerge and flowers continue appearing for a month or more. The flowers never go through an unsightly stage because of the quick petal release. Many gardeners shy away from Foetida

Rosa foetida bicolor growing in our back garden

Bicolor's intense coloring, but with imaginative planting, she adds great pizzazz to a spring garden.

Foetida Bicolor is a most exciting companion in the vase. I like to harvest buds and watch them open in the house. The flower lasts only a day. Her fallen petals are a unique accessory—they highlight the fragile, fleeting opulence this rose offers creation.

I have no qualms about including her in a lush bouquet of roses. Her coloring and simple form are a thrilling harmonizer.

The name of this dazzling rose doesn't do her justice, but her initial, *F*, endowed my alphabet with the rose I wanted to include most of all.

Above: A small cluster glows in a bud vase. **Opposite**: Brilliant Foetida Bicolor blooms add drama when mixed with fluffy pastel roses.

graham thomas

GRAHAM THOMAS

A Chinese vase displays a formal arrangement of 'Graham Thomas' inserted into a base of spiraea and hypericum.

In the early 1990s, four names began to filter through my rose world with puzzling frequency: 'Graham Thomas', Graham Stuart Thomas, David Austin, and English Roses. It took several years before I realized that 'Graham Thomas', the prolific golden rose in my garden, was called an English Rose. Then I found out that David Austin, who I introduce in the next chapter, created English Roses. But who was Graham Stuart Thomas? He was the man in love with roses and the namesake for my alphabet's *G*.

Mr. Thomas immediately endeared himself to me when I read, "I think the rose must hold a high place in our early affection for flowers. I can distinctly remember delighting in the fragrance of the Hybrid Perpetual 'Mrs. John Laing' at the age of eight…".

Born in Cambridge, England, in 1909, Graham remembers each rose that he came in contact with and writes about them in his epic history of roses, *The Graham Stuart Thomas*

Rose Book. When he states that he lost his heart to the sight of the Gallica 'Belle de Crécy' growing next to the Damask rose 'Mme Hardy', one of my personal favorites, I lost my heart to Mr. Thomas. Reading the account of his life's path fascinated me. Seeing those two roses in 1937 ignited a curiosity, which led him on a serendipitous journey to find out all he could about Antique Roses.

In a span of over thirty years that included World War II, Thomas found and chronicled most all of the existing Antique Roses: the Gallicas, Damasks, Albas, Centifolias, and Mosses. The richly scented blooms of these roses are mostly pink;

Graham Thomas photographed by Susan as we toured his garden. His namesake rose is in his buttonhole and growing in the background.

a few, like 'Mme Hardy', are white, while the Gallicas include deep pinks, crimsons, and rich violets. These once-blooming garden shrubs fell from favor when the China Roses began to have an impact on the hybridizing of repeat-bloomers. As the overwhelmingly popular Hybrid Teas came into fashion, these antique jewels of the garden were quickly fazed out. The group became known as "Old Roses" once they had disappeared from the marketplace.

Graham and other kindred souls weren't about to let them disappear. He hunted for these

SMELLING LIKE FRESH TEA ROSES, CUPPED BLOOMS ON LONG ARCHING STEMS ARE FRIENDLY AND EAGER TO BE WORKED WITH IN FLOWER ARRANGING.

Old Roses, shrub by shrub, growing in near, distant, and secret gardens throughout England, France, Germany, and the United States. When people heard of his interest, invitations to rose sites appeared just when the roses happened to be blooming. By the 1950s Graham Thomas made his Old Rose collection available to world commerce by reintroducing them through his work at nurseries in England.

His work also included searching every plant treatise, herbal, gardening book, and catalog of the past. He painstakingly culled, documented, and reworked the history of roses. In the process, he

'Graham Thomas' (the rose) in my garden

became the world's most knowledgeable rosarian. He studied in the University Botanic Garden in Cambridge and wrote seventeen books extolling roses and other garden subjects. At age fifty, in need of illustrations for his books, he became an accom-plished horticultural artist. He created an exquisite portfolio of line drawings, pencil renderings, and watercolors. In 1974, he became Garden Adviser to England's National Trust.

Graham Thomas designed lavish gardens on

ten of the National Trust properties. The rose garden at Mottisfont Abbey contains Thomas's collection of more than 350 pre-1900 roses.

After researching and drafting this chapter, I had the chance to visit Mottisfont and the privilege of meeting Graham Thomas at Briar Cottage, his home in Surrey.

The original building at Mottisfont was a priory built in 1201. Graham transformed two sections of a three-part kitchen garden into a stunning showcase for his rose collection. Ancient brick walls surrounding the gardens are blanketed with carefully trained climbing roses. Both gardens, which cover about one-and-a-half acres, have a formal structure built around a central axis. Simple square wood arches and rustic supports, strategically placed, overflow with fanciful ramblers. Graham masterfully planted the roses to complement their personalities and underplanted them with great pastel drifts of perennials.

On the day of our meeting, Mr. Thomas warmly welcomed my friend Susan and me into his lovely, art-filled cottage. Over coffee and cookies, Susan and I gave him a report on the roses we had just seen at Mottisfont. It was marvelous to look into his happy, light blue eyes and tell him about other gardens we had seen—Nymans, Hidcote, Kiftsgate, Sissinghurst, Cothay Manor, Hadspen. He reminisced about his rose-searching days and showed us artwork on the walls created by both his mother and father. He told us that during his time managing Sunningdale Nursery, the business expanded from 25 to 110 acres.

'Graham Thomas', the only modern rose at Mottisfont

'Lauré Davoust' climbs an arch amongst an extravagant planting of roses and perennials at the rose garden designed by Graham Thomas at Mottisfont Abbey.

'Graham Thomas' climbs a wall at Brook Cottage, a garden we visited in England.

About the young David Austin, Graham said, "When he really started collecting, he came to see me and fell in love with the roses as I did, and before I knew it, he was making his own."

Years later, Austin gave Graham the honor of choosing a rose to be his namesake. He told us, "The rose I chose was the one and only yellow rose in a field of roses the size of a football field."

Since Graham was ninety-two, I asked him if he would like me to read a draft of this chapter to him. I wanted his approval and hoped to correct any mistakes. He said, "No, I'll read it."

He read faster than I did! He liked what I had to say, told me I misspelled

Abbey, and suggested I do away with formality in the text and call him Graham.

Afterwards, he gave us a tour of his handsome garden, pointing out numerous shrubs, vines, perennials, and roses. He paused by 'Mlle Cécile Brünner' and said, "Exquisite bud, lovely little thing, just right for a buttonhole." When Graham goes out he likes to wear a rose on his lapel.

Back inside, he showed us his book-lined study. At his direction, we took the enormous rose history volumes by Redouté and Miss Willmott from the shelves and leafed through the beautiful rose images that he so tirelessly used in his research.

Now I want to tell you about the rose named after him. Introduced in 1983, 'Graham Thomas' is a cross between 'Iceberg' and 'Charles Austin'. One bloom period can produce fifty to sixty stems! In my garden, the shrub becomes six feet tall—if you refrain from pruning the shrub it will grow into a climber. It is also wonderfully heat-resistant and the shrub looks very impressive in the garden. Smelling like fresh Tea roses, cupped blooms on long arching stems are friendly and eager to be worked with in flower arranging.

David Austin eloquently gives Graham Stuart Thomas credit for paving the way to English Roses. It is interesting that Graham chose a yellow rose for his namesake. There were almost no yellow roses amongst his beloved Antiques. His choice respectfully supports the fascinating progress of today's rose hybrids and the remarkable work of David Austin.

So many roses are named after people; I wish

I knew who they were. It was a great honor to meet and be in the presence of this rose's namesake. Graham Thomas thought my alphabet was a very exciting project. He said, "No one has ever done this before; I am honored to be the *G*." Graham Stuart Thomas died on April 16, 2003.

How did all these roses fit into the narrow neck of this Portuguese vase? Floral foam does the trick. (See Arranging Roses, page 200.)

HERITAGE

'Heritage' has many sisters in the same color range. Bunched together in a large arrangement are 'Heritage', 'Cressida', 'Tamora', 'Sweet Juliet', 'Belle Story', 'English Garden', and 'Canterbury'.

As I prepared to write this chapter, my friend Susan and I were examining English Roses in her back garden. We each plucked several fragrant blooms and laid them on a table to admire. As Susan fingered the pale petals of 'Eglantine', she said, "Look what David Austin has done." We marveled at the roses before us and about how they have added so much beauty to our lives.

During the past fifty years, David Austin dreamed up and bred a whole new race of roses. 'Heritage', my alphabet's *H*, is among the 150 creations of this passionate rose lover.

As a teenager, David Austin was more interested in propagating roses than tending potatoes and barley on his father's farm in Albrighton, England. He had no idea that one day his inherited fields would yield crops of roses. The transformation began after World War II when David purchased an Old Rose named 'Stanwell Perpetual'. He was fascinated that a chance crossing had endowed the fragrant shrub of pale pink blooms with a repeat-flowering habit, and it occurred to him that nature's crossing could be duplicated using modern methods. In his spare time, he began researching cross-pollination.

THE IDEAL BEAUTY AND COLOR AUSTIN SAW IN 'BELLE ISIS' SO MANY YEARS AGO IS UNCANNILY CAPTURED IN THE GRACEFUL CUPPED FLOWERS OF 'HERITAGE'.

Austin dreamed of breeding roses that retained the heady fragrance of Old Roses. He also wanted to combine the charming cupped, rosette, and cabbage bloom shapes of the Old Roses with the newer colors and the repeat-flowering of modern roses.

When he began to dabble in hybridizing, his rewards were immediate. Austin says luck was on his side when he chose the parents of his first progeny—

A repoussé sugar bowl is a captivating container for 'Heritage'.

the Gallica of blush pink rosettes named 'Belle Isis' and 'Dainty Maid', a Floribunda of pink singles.

He carefully brushed the pollen collected from one parent onto the stigma of the other. With great excitement, he watched as pollinated hips began to swell and ripen with seed. He planted the seeds and waited for them to germinate. He knew every seed would produce a mixture of the parent's characteristics and that each seedling would be unique. When the seeds developed into plants and began blooming, Austin noticed one spectacular specimen that stood out from the rest. The plant's clear-pink bloom had all the qualities he loved—it was fragrant, luxurious, and almost the size of a peony. To his surprise, the rose looked nothing like its parents, but it had the alluring myrrh fragrance of 'Belle Isis'.

As he watched the development of the cuttings budded to rootstock, he was thrilled by their vigor and trained them into both ample shrubs and gloriously sprawling climbers. Austin named his first hybrid 'Constance Spry', after the English floral designer famous for her inventive use of flowers. Constance was also a keen collector of Old Roses. Graham Thomas introduced Austin's first hybrid to the public at Sunningdale Nursery in 1961. 'Constance Spry' is now a classic rose and a great commercial success.

Even though 'Constance Spry' had all the characteristics Austin dreamed of, she did not rebloom. However in his book, *David Austin's English Roses*, he goes into detail about how her genes went on to become the early foundation of

time, he is also dreaming up next April's crosses and keeping abreast of worldwide production, distribution, and marketing. Michael says David is absolutely amazed that his hobby became a world-famous enterprise.

As we walked through the garden, Michael plucked roses for us to smell. He helped us distinguish fragrances—myrrh, cloves, musk, strawberry. In one of the fields, Michael pointed out more roses that would be discarded. Incredulous, I said, "David Austin, the man who threw away billions of roses . . ." Michael finished my sentence, ". . . in search of perfection."

Thanks to David Austin's quest, my alphabet has a *G*, *T*, *H*, and an *R*—a surprise discovery I will introduce further on.

Bunched together in a large arrangement are 'Heritage', 'Cressida', 'Tamora', 'Sweet Juliet', 'Belle Story', 'English Garden', and 'Evelyn'.

iceberg

ICEBERG

How could I possibly represent the world's most popular rose on one vertical line? 'Iceberg's' skinny initial abbreviates her brilliance. Not only is 'Iceberg' a breeding parent to the English Roses 'Graham Thomas' and 'Heritage', she is a prolific and constant bloomer. She's also a key player in landscape design and flower arranging.

Introduced in 1958, 'Iceberg' is a Floribunda raised by W. Kordes. Her parents were 'Virgo', the most admired white Hybrid Tea of her day, and a frisky red Polyantha named 'Robin Hood'.

During the 1860s, at the Guillot nursery in France, a multiflora (cluster flowering) rose that had recently come from Japan exchanged pollen with a hybrid rose imported from China. Small, sturdy, cluster-flowering shrubs that bloomed continuously were the result, and they were classified as Polyanthas. Fifty years later, breeders began crossing Polyantha genes with other rose families. They gradually developed shrubs that flowered more abundantly and were hardier than Hybrid Teas. This new class of roses became known as Floribundas, and 'Iceberg' is its most renowned member. Rose gardeners and landscape professionals alike wish they could have one like her in every color.

Two roses that grow in my garden influenced 'Iceberg's' lineage: 'Pâquerette', the first Polyantha, and her Japanese parent, *R. multiflora*. Lined up beside

THIS ROSE WILL SPOIL A BEGINNER. THE FRAGRANT ROSE SPRAYS ARE SUPPORTED BY DOZENS OF LONG, ELEGANT, AND ALMOST THORNLESS STEMS.

'Iceberg', below, they clearly show the progression of cluster-flowering. 'Robin Hood's' strong Polyantha traits endowed 'Iceberg' with continuous masses of bloom. 'Virgo' supplied structure and color.

Cut stems of *R. multiflora* and the Polyantha 'Pâquerette' next to 'Iceberg' show the genetic influence of clustered blooms.

'Iceberg's' inheritance also includes a handsome shrub form, densely clothed with light green shiny leaves and beautiful flower buds often blushed with pink.

Russell Page, the renowned English landscape designer, was the first to see the value of 'Iceberg'. He planted her en masse in many of his gardens in the 1960s and 1970s. His signature of bedding 'Iceberg' with boxwood edging has become a classic garden statement. In England, we saw this treatment in Vita Sackville-West's white garden at Sissinghurst.

Since 'Iceberg' is such a wonderful repeat bloomer, she is a great garden asset. Her white flowers brighten and highlight garden spaces. I've seen the shrub variety lining walkways, bordering a flagstone terrace, and encircling trees. Budded onto tall stems, they make wonderful standards, and you can also find a climbing form, fit for clambering over trees and pergolas. 'Iceberg' roses meld beautifully with Old, Modern, and English Roses.

'Iceberg's' prolific nature can make her daunting to prune. Try not to get lost in the network of upper branches. Start low, at least one-half or two-thirds down. You can't make a mistake on 'Iceberg'. She'll regrow and bloom no matter what.

This rose will spoil a beginner. The fragrant rose sprays are supported by dozens of long, elegant, and almost thornless stems. Also, since the buds don't open all at once, 'Iceberg' has an extensive bloom period. When I finally remove the last spent blooms, new red leaves are already popping out of bud-eyes for the next growth cycle!

'Iceberg' standards planted in a semicircle and edged in boxwood make a dynamic statement.

With only one or two 'Iceberg' rosebushes, you can fashion wonderful large arrangements. The best time to harvest long stems is after the large central bud (leader) in the spray has bloomed and a few more buds have their sepals naturally pulled back.

The rest of the buds will open in the warmth of the house, adding enchantment to an arrangement for days.

'Iceberg' might stimulate the wedding designer in you. You don't have to be a florist; lovely bridal

bouquets are easy to make. I like to work out ideas with the blooms from my two shrubs. If you have an 'Iceberg', try making a bridal bouquet; you'll see how easy it is.

In June of 2000, our friends Dot Carhart and Owen Cooper asked if they could be married in our back garden by the 'Cécile Brünner' arch. Six guests, poetic vows, and our garden were all the couple wanted. They didn't even think of a bridal bouquet—but I did.

On the morning of the wedding, I went to one of my 'Icebergs' and clipped about a dozen short stems into my hand. I knew Dot liked columbine; I added several white ones along with a few lavender sweet peas. Then I wrapped floral tape high up around the stems, recut all the stems under water, tied a gauzy white

'Iceberg' underplanted with catmint in my garden along the front sidewalk

bow around them, and placed the bouquet in a glass of water to await Dot's arrival. After making a boutonniere for Owen, we were ready for what turned out to be a day of delight. Later, Dot's bouquet, perched in a water glass, decorated our luncheon table overlooking the San Francisco Bay at the romantic Claremont Hotel.

My 'Icebergs' are sometimes still going strong in December. With the shrubs full of buds in 1998, I anticipated making wonderful Christmas bouquets; I even hoped to decorate the tree with the white roses. A heavy frost came a week before Christmas and the roses were gone in flash. But the next year I gathered a big bouquet of 'Icebergs' on Christmas day! I gleefully filled the gift of an antique crystal rose vase I opened from my husband that morning. I didn't have to wait until spring to see how perfectly the vase displayed the lovely blooms.

In the world of roses, 'Iceberg' is matchless; her initial shows only a hint of her true nature.

Three bridal bouquets illustrate handheld arranging and different design treatments. Here, 'Iceberg' and abelia stems were cut at various lengths for a pointed handle.

Here, the stems were cut short and straight across to use as a fringe above a wrap of satin ribbon. The ribbon is folded and tacked in place with straight pins.

Here, sweet peas and 'Iceberg' stems make a thicker graduated handle. A bow with long streamers was added after wrapping and pinning the handle.

JUST JOEY

Fully open blooms grace an interior setting; the painting of orchids in the background is by my husband, Leroy Parker.

Roses have become the symbols of many of my life's most precious memories. When I see or think of 'Just Joey' there is a tapestry of recollection.

"Carolyn do you have a picture of a Joey rose?" my friend Marilou asked over the phone on an evening in November.

"Do you mean 'Just Joey'?" I replied.

She wasn't sure and told me that at lunch that day she happened to sit next to a woman who was searching for a photograph of a peach-colored rose named "Joey something."

I told Marilou about a beautiful close-up portrait I had taken of the rose 'Just Joey', which hung on my living room wall in a gold-leaf frame.

Encouraged by this news, Marilou went on to tell me that her new acquaintance had a three-year-old nephew, named Joey, who had died of a sudden illness several days before.

The woman thought since her sister grew 'Just Joey' roses in her garden, she might be comforted by a gift of a beautiful picture of the rose in memory of her son.

IN A WAY, HER NAME SUBTLY ACKNOWLEDGES THAT SHE IS "JUST" ONE OF THE MOST BEAUTIFUL HYBRID TEAS IN THE WORLD TODAY.

Thanks to Marilou's heartfelt resourcefulness, I made contact with the woman. I was touched by her endeavor and happy that I could fulfill her wish so easily. She purchased my photo of 'Just Joey' and gave it to her sister just three days later.

Opulent blooms complement a nasturtium-patterned vase by Leroy Parker.

Roger Pawsey, an English hybridizer, named his rose 'Just Joey' as a loving tribute to his wife. Introduced in England in 1972, 'Just Joey' took ten years to make it across the Atlantic. Once here she created an immediate sensation.

'Just Joey' is the first Hybrid Tea to bloom in my spring garden. I like to lose myself in 'Just Joey' for she is a breathtaking rose. A distinctive swirling center opens frilled petals to form magnificent blooms smelling of roses and apricots. My shrub took a number of years to establish good form but always bloomed by the armload. 'Just Joey's' new maroon leaves have a tendency to mildew, and her stems tend to be slightly crooked. It doesn't bother me—she has one of the prettiest rose faces I know.

'Just Joey's' color did not even exist in roses until the twentieth century. When Pernet-Ducher unlocked the genes of the Foetidas, he not only bequeathed us reblooming yellow roses, but apricot and peach roses too.

Over the years, my friend Sandy had asked me several times for the names of good peach roses to grow, so I felt she must have a specific love for them.

One Saturday morning, our friend Bill called to tell us that people were gathering in a nearby parking lot in fifteen minutes to give our friend Sandy a loving send-off. She was flying to Germany for cancer treatment. I thanked Bill for the call, grabbed my clippers and rushed into the garden.

I cut single stems of 'Brandy', 'Apricot Nectar', 'Smooth Angel', and 'Just Joey', all my favorite peach roses. In the kitchen, I reclipped their stems under water and wrapped a soaking wet paper towel around them. Then I enclosed the posy in a plastic sandwich bag wound with a rubber band, attached a cheery peach bow, and hurried out the door to my car.

In the parking lot, people surrounded Sandy's car. I thrust the small, fragrant bouquet through the car window into her hands amidst the waves, hugs, and kisses of many loving friends.

'Just Joey' lies on paper made by my husband, Leroy. Several days after Sandy's memorial service, he gathered rose petals from the floral creations sent for her and embedded them in paper as special mementos for Sandy's family and friends.

A posy, like the one I gave to Sandy, wrapped with a wet paper towel and enclosed in a plastic sandwich bag.

What a face!

Later, I found out how much the little posy meant to Sandy—her husband, Jim, told me the roses lasted for four days in her hospital room in Germany. Sandy passed away two months after her treatment, and fortunately I had more opportunities to give her peach roses. She in turn showered me with love and memories of the deepest kind.

When I tell people 'Just Joey's' name, it always confuses the conversation. In a way, her name subtly acknowledges that she is "just" one of the most beautiful Hybrid Teas in the world today, a regal *J* in this alphabet.

KATHLEEN

'Kathleen' in a carnival glass dish, the "poor man's" Tiffany glass

My years of gardening have been blessed with special friendships. Mary Beale Knowles has shared every phase with me.

In 1989, our relationship blossomed when I asked if I might visit her garden. In my new, ex-fashion-designer mode, I was searching for shrubs that could be used for greens in rose arranging. Mary, who is a landscape designer, made suggestions as she took me on a wonderful tour of her free-flowing, cottage-style garden. Before I left, she lent me two anthologies written by English women gardeners.

Thoroughly captivated, I read the books from cover to cover. It didn't matter that the women spoke of vast estates and mentioned scores of plants by their Latin names. I wanted to garden like they did. I soon became a plant collector and began styling my garden in new ways.

Mary and I turned out to be frequent companions. We visit gardens, go to seminars, lunch, and shop bookstores and nurseries together. With a great sense of adventure, Mary always drives. On our plant quests we have humorously found ourselves lost on the winding roads of northern California's backcountry. One time, a rainstorm marooned us overnight on the Mendocino Coast.

Mary's mother, Eve, nurtured her daughter's wonderful, free spirit. Nature adventures were a pivotal aspect of Mary's childhood. In an old car hooked up with a trailer, Eve often took Mary, her four brothers, and their cat on camping trips up and down California and into Mexico. Along the way, they gathered little treasures and put them on display in the two vehicles—leaves, seedpods, crystals, rocks, flowers....

Mary told me about the rose, 'Kathleen', that her mother had grown from a small piece of rose cane obtained at a cutting-and-seed swap. I met Eve's 'Kathleen' on one of our journeys. Mary and I stopped by her mother's home in Santa Rosa

BEFORE US, IN FULL-BLOOM, 'KATHLEEN' GLORIFIED TEN FEET OF FENCING ALONG A NARROW COURTYARD. TRUSSES OF PINK BUDS AND BLUSH-WHITE FLOWERS THAT RESEMBLE APPLE BLOSSOMS BUBBLED FROM A STURDY WELL-BRANCHED TRUNK.

to pot up summer annuals for her. When we walked out to the back porch, I stood there agog. Before us, in full-bloom, 'Kathleen' glorified ten feet of fencing along a narrow courtyard. Trusses of peach buds and blush-pink flowers that resemble apple blossoms bubbled from a sturdy well-branched trunk.

'Kathleen', a Hybrid Musk that grows from seven to fifteen feet, was introduced by Reverend Joseph Pemberton in 1922. Jack Harkness, the English hybridizer, says the Musk Rose is more like a remote ancestor to this group. Pemberton did not keep accurate records, but employed the resources of many roses to produce this wonderful group of small-flowered shrubs. Hybrid Musks have become irreplaceable to the garden designer because their naturally graceful growth requires little upkeep.

As a new shrub, 'Kathleen' in training to climb a signpost at our side garden

'Kathleen' in hand-blown glass bowls signed Louis Comfort Tiffany—a study in opulence and simplicity

'Kathleen' has an upright healthy habit, a good repeat bloom, and a spicy-sweet fragrance. Her leaf-padded canes are thornless and generously add structure to a bouquet like the one on the left, making floral foam or a frog unnecessary for arranging. Her long leaflets of coppery new growth add interesting texture to the garden. I have found, however, that during a heat wave, without the right amount of moisture in the ground, new leaf tips will bake to a crisp.

You can prune 'Kathleen' with something as rough as a hedge trimmer to suit the size and shape you desire. I clip off unproductive wood and trim off the hips to promote more blooms.

When Mary and I finished the potting that day, Mary's mother, Eve, gave us a tour of her home's inner gardens. There are three courtyards in all. The roses beamed with a rare beauty and contentment in Eve's care amidst a wonderful mélange of perennials and shrubs. I particularly liked her decorative plantings of blueberry bushes and Japanese maples.

Later, sitting in her rich, almost baroque parlor, my eyes continually soothed themselves on a rose Eve had placed in a small leaf-shape bowl. Sitting on a console across the room, the pink bloom welcomed me and spoke of Eve's love of creation and her life.

Mary told me her mother always has flowers or seasonal branches intimately placed in her home. I am moved when a person takes time to provide themselves with nature's gifts. I retain such images; they nurture my consciousness. Simple acts with

'Kathleen' clusters in a small dish

flowers radiate love and positive energy in a circumference that has no bounds.

I joined Mary and her mother at a cutting and seed swap a few years later. Each guest is invited to share her garden's riches. From my garden, I gathered and labeled rose cuttings, unusual ivy specimens, and cream California poppy seeds.

In a large, private garden in Sonoma, we were treated to a buffet lunch with an interesting and vital group of gardeners. Afterwards, I delighted in helping myself to nigella and Shirley poppy seeds. Then I perused and chose cuttings that were set in buckets in a cool, wooded area. Not only did my garden's assets increase, I met kindred spirits and learned new ideas during an inventive and fulfilling afternoon.

Looking like apple blossoms, branches of 'Kathleen' are inserted into a cylindrical vase.

The mobility of cuttings and seeds is a perk for dedicated gardeners. Just yesterday, from my friend Susan's black hollyhocks, I brought home a fat, papery pouch ripe with a ring of big, round, charcoal-colored seeds.

Once I asked my Uncle Norm to send me cuttings of wild roses from his woodland garden in Oregon. His rose cuttings came in the mail in the most interesting package I have ever received. I eagerly tore away brown wrapping paper to find a shoebox lined in clear plastic. The forest floor—old leaves, lichen, fresh green moss, fir needles, earth, and even an earthworm—protected cuttings and rooted suckers. In the spring, Oregon's variation of pink wild roses bloomed in my garden.

Thanks to Eve, my alphabet has a superb *K* and 'Kathleen' reminded me of the joy of friendship, the magic of internal communion, and the miracle of procreation.

A 'Kathleen' arrangement in the garden

LILAC CHARM

The rim on this pedestal plate allows just enough water for an elegant floating display.

Mother's Day is famously rosy. Nurseries are well stocked with blooming, potted roses for mom, and rosarians hold fetes and celebrations for her.

In our second year at our Lafayette home, my family took me on a Mother's Day rose outing to Roses of Yesterday and Today. Francis E. Lester founded the mail-order business near Watsonville, California, in the 1930s. Lester's partner and successor, Will Tillotson, corresponded and shared cuttings with Graham Stuart Thomas. The company's goal was to compile and market an ideal rose collection of three hundred varieties, old and new.

For years, I had been charmed by the inventive rose descriptions in their annual catalog. One admirer sent Tillotson a letter telling him that reading the catalog every evening before bed soothed her to sleep.

With an invitation to a Mother's Day Open House, we drove on country roads bordered by fields and forests. When we reached Brown's Valley Road, a row of gold and crimson Foetida Bicolor roses along a fence leading to the display garden indicated that we were in for a rose extravaganza.

Still a neophyte to the expansive world of roses, I was bowled over by huge ramblers and climbers brimming with blooms. Petite shrubs, voluptuous Rugosas, Bourbons, Albas, Gallicas, Teas, and Hybrid Teas, even the yellow *Rosa foetida*, all bloomed in a surround of towering redwoods.

Though Roses of Yesterday and Today is primarily a bare root business, on Mother's Day roses are potted up for sale. That day, I received as gifts

'Lilac Charm' and 'Intrigue', in floral foam, embellish a fanciful soap dish.

from my family my first 'Iceberg', the luscious shell pink 'Gruss an Aachen', and 'Lilac Charm', my alphabet's *L*.

A Floribunda of singles introduced by Edward Burton Le Grice in 1961, 'Lilac Charm' was my first unusual rose. Her striking lilac petals revealing magenta stamens and gold anthers were irresistible and unique. Only two feet high and up to four feet wide, she's been blooming in our garden for fifteen years. With a

IN SEARCH OF MY OWN UNDERSTANDING, I FOUND THAT THE SINGLE ROSES WERE TELLING ME THAT LIFE WITHIN US IS AS BEAUTIFUL AND GLOWING AS A SINGLE ROSE'S MAGNIFICENT CENTER.

sweet clovey fragrance, the disease-resistant shrub repeats almost as quickly as 'Iceberg'. Her low growth habit makes a lovely planting at the front of a border. In arrangements, her short stems limit her use. In a medium-size mixed bouquet, she would do well placed at the front edge of the vase.

Ten years later, I returned to Roses of Yesterday and Today to photograph other single roses. There were so many—each variety exceptional.

Single roses have had a strong impact on my life. When I was twenty-four, I took a hike with companions in Marin County, California. We began on a path through a sunny field high with fresh waving grasses and wildflowers. Soon we entered a deep, dark redwood forest. On a narrow path, there were people in front of me and behind me, but I felt alone in that awesome space. The sun's rays wove through the soaring trunks and filtered through lacy branches. My eye landed on a fluttering white shape caught in a ray of sunlight. I saw an open, five-petaled wild rose with a bursting center of golden stamens. The small white flower courageously revealed its glowing inner core in an ecstasy of self-giving.

In those early days, I had more meetings of similar impact with single roses. When I gave birth to my first baby, I nursed her in a rocking chair next to a window with a view of 'Irish Fireflame'. I didn't know the rose's name at the time, but she thrilled me as I watched her surge through a bank of junipers with long, pointed, coral buds that opened into big peach singles. New love of creation nourished by motherhood and this rose inspired me to order the Roses of Yesterday and Today catalog, which I had seen advertised in the back of a gardening magazine. I didn't become a rose gardener until years later, but reading the descriptions fulfilled an internal creativity.

The catalog's founder Frances Lester also wrote a book, *My Friend the Rose*, published in 1942, in which he celebrates the rose lover's garden:

It is a bit of Nature that reflects the taste of its owner, a sounding-board on which to practice one's understanding of growing plants; it may even be a well-spring for a new philosophy of life. Any garden may be this, especially if planted with the flowers one most loves.

In search of my own understanding, I found that the single roses were telling me that life within us is as beautiful and glowing as a single rose's magnificent center. When I saw 'Lilac Charm', this inner truth awakened within me once again.

People think lasting qualities can sometimes be an issue with singles. On the contrary, many singles easily last for several days and should be picked in bud or, if open, in the morning when the anthers are fresh. They are delightful additions to a bouquet. For a gift, I like to add buds of singles to a mixed bouquet and let the recipient be surprised by their opening.

However long their life is, each rose, from a bramble to a Hybrid Tea, has a stimulating experience to offer anyone who chooses to gather, display, and admire her presence. Next to my computer, as I write, sits an intensely fragrant, purplish magenta single called 'News'. All day, the glow of her petal color has deepened to tones of darker purple and Chianti as her rich gold center has remained poised and tranquil. Plucked yesterday, gone tomorrow, I am richer after witnessing her evolution.

The rose gifts I received on my first trip to Roses of Yesterday and Today were a great success in the garden and helped my husband and me realize that we had room for a multitude of roses. The next winter, I wore out their catalog reading descriptions of roses over and over again. I finally compiled a list and ordered thirty different rosebushes to climb and border a new fence for the side garden that faces the school across the street.

I'm pleased that 'Lilac Charm' gave me a chance to mention motherhood and my experiences with one of the world's unique rose purveyors. It is a joy to share the beauty and my love of single roses.

'Eglantine'

'White Rose of York'

Rosa rubrifolia glauca

'Golden Wings'

'Complicata'

'Paulii'

'Lilac Charm' has many single rose companions. Here are just a few that I photographed at Roses of Yesterday and Today.

MOSS ROSE

A clutch of short-stemmed Moss Roses graces a footed vase.

Our neighbor Tony La Rosa noticed that my husband and I had an insatiable appetite for roses. One day he brought over a bundle of thin, well-rooted rose canes telling us, "My mother has been growing this rose for years; I thought you might like it for your garden."

He went on to say, "When a fellow who worked in the deli of our family's grocery store visited Italy, he brought cuttings of this rose back home stuck in a potato." Tony didn't know the name of the rose.

I was touched by his gift and excited by the new addition to our roses. I watched closely the next spring as unusually airy, well-defined leaves began to sprout and take form. Short delicate hairs covered thin, graceful stems. When buds began to show, they were liberally laced with moss! The curiously tactile bundles had a scent like pine needles and peaches. I watched the fancy buds open to expose a tight sheath of deep pink. The petal soon paled as it released a full rosette whose beauty took my breath away. I sighed as the luscious expansion revealed a stunningly fragrant bloom. Silky inner petals curled around a tiny tuft of pale yellow stamens.

I found out that this heartthrob of a rose is named 'Common Moss'. Far from

I WATCHED THE FANCY BUDS OPEN TO EXPOSE A TIGHT SHEATH OF DEEP PINK. THE PETAL SOON PALED AS IT RELEASED A FULL ROSETTE WHOSE BEAUTY TOOK MY BREATH AWAY.

In full bloom, 'Common Moss' shows her lavish display in a Chinese clay pot.

common, she was discovered in the south of France at Carcassonne, as far back as 1696, and is thought to be a sport of *Rosa centifolia*. She is the only rose in my alphabet that joined the treasures in Empress Josephine's rose garden at Malmaison, her country estate in Reuil, now a suburb of Paris.

I'll tell you more about the admirable characteristics of 'Common Moss' after I mention that we have Josephine to thank for the dawn of the rose's popularity. In 1799, before Josephine dispatched botanists and plant hunters to gather the world's rose specimens, the ranunculus was the most popular flower in Europe! Sixty-five years earlier, Carolus Linnaeus, Swedish botanist and founder of the modern classification system for plants and animals, listed only twenty known roses. In less than ten years, Josephine and her assistants amassed and even hybridized more than 250 varieties of roses and countless other plant species. As the wife of Napoleon, Josephine's plant hunters had carte blanche to his ships. Special arrangements even allowed carriers of roses to pass through an English blockade during the Napoleonic Wars.

Josephine, fortunately supported by her husband's royal wealth, commissioned extensive gardens to show off the horticultural bounty. There are receipts, lists, and contracts regarding botanical business verifying that Malmaison became Europe's leading center of botanical research during her reign. Roger Phillips and Martyn Rix, in *The Quest for the Rose*, say she exchanged plants with botanic gardens and shared her discoveries with nurserymen. The now classic rose and plant studies she

'Common Moss' in her first stage of bloom

commissioned Redouté to paint attest to the magnificence of her collection. Redouté's precise renderings were crucial to historical and botanical research in the years to come.

I can barely imagine a more exhausting life than Josephine's. She survived hurricanes, ignorance, poverty, prison, betrayal, battles, wars, inability to produce an heir, abandonment, divorce, hatred, jealousy, and scorn. Yet she was greatly loved by people in all walks of life. Her elegant and

'Common Moss' bud

gentle manner, love of beauty, and sense of style remained intact throughout.

Josephine inspired and commissioned designs for everything from gardens and courtly chambers to satin slippers. She set the style of the day and for years to come. I can imagine how she loved 'Common Moss'. I'm sure she placed the fragrant blooms at the décolleté necklines of her infamously sheer gowns. On at least one occasion, she had real rose petals stitched to her costume.

Josephine's love of roses and genuine knowledge of plants must have been nurtured in her childhood on her parent's sugar plantation in Martinique. Josephine was full of life, and her spirit triumphed in roses. After her death in 1814, her garden at Malmaison fell into disrepair, but the legacy of her roses went on to thrive in the hands of French nurserymen. Throughout the nineteenth century, they reigned supreme as the producers of the best roses, which were exported and grown all over the world.

'Common Moss' derives her individuality from sticky glandular growths that look like moss attached to the buds. In his book, *Roses*, horticulturist Jack Harkness says, "Why these growths should so concentrate in one area is a mystery. It is perhaps a chance shuffling of the rose's resources."

Moss Roses bloom only once. Our Moss Rose is one of the highlights of our spring season. The three-foot-tall shrub has suckering roots with a contained, neat habit. The roots don't travel like the Gallicas and Rugosas; they stay concentrated to one spot. By digging up a mass of canes, I can easily pull apart numerous plants, all bearing their own roots. In England, at Kew Gardens, I saw 'Common Moss' budded to rootstock. The shrub sorely lacked the personality of the natural version.

I first planted the canes Tony gave us three feet away from our western-exposed side fence. The buds and stems had a tendency to mildew, but I later realized that the fence and a large tree blocked out the sun until noon and inhibited air circulation. Roses don't like to wait so long to feel the sun's rays. The plants did much better when I moved them to more open ground.

The roots of 'Common Moss' go deep into the ground. I noticed that the spot where I removed the canes continued to issue forth shoots of new plants. I

The thin stems of 'Common Moss' allow the use of narrow-necked vases in arrangements.

decided to encourage their development. I now use the site to dig up new canes, and like Tony did, give them to people who would appreciate such rare beauty.

Seven years ago, the graceful shape and small size of 'Common Moss' inspired me to plant a few canes in a pair of Chinese clay pots. With only one dose of fertilizer a year and no repotting, they overflow with splendor each spring. When the

blooms finish, I prune the shrubs way back (both those in pots and in the ground). Handsome new leaves soon appear. If the leaves get mildew, I cut them back again, knowing they will soon refresh themselves. In the winter, aside from more cutting back, I sometimes cut old wood to decongest the thicket of stems.

Both Tony La Rosa and Empress Josephine (born Marie-Joseph Rose Tacher de la Pagerie) share the name Rose. I'm indebted to each of them for my alphabet's lovely *M*.

Pots of 'Common Moss', already pruned back, sit in front of a row of the shrubs displaying their last blooms. On the ground rooted canes are ready to be potted.

'Common Moss' in a small silver bowl

nevada

NEVADA

A poem by Tennyson circles this antique pewter rose bowl by Archibald Knox for Liberty of London.

Through the years, I've identified myself with particular roses. In 1980, I was the dramatic, passionate Foetida Bicolor (page 46); in 1987, the bliss-drunk 'Sweet Surrender' (page 134). In 2000, 'Nevada' was my soul's happiness. 'Nevada' embodies the last two lines of a poem given to me while I was collecting poetry for my first book.

My old friend Thea stopped her car when she saw me watering the front rose bed. "Carolyn," she called through her open window, "I found a great rose excerpt in a poem by Shelley; you might want it for your book."

And the rose like a nymph to the bath addressed,
Which unveiled the depth of her glowing breast,
Till, fold after fold, to the fainting air
The soul of her beauty and love lay bare;

PERCY BYSSCHE SHELLEY, 1792–1822

Even though this poem seems overembellished, I couldn't get it out of my mind. The last two lines, in particular, always seem to resonate within me, and I find myself repeating them.

Only one bloom-filled stem, with its decorative, high-set leaves, in a Roseville vase

After several of these poetic visitations, I thought, *This poem must be about me—my depth, beauty, and love.* Beauty affects us all deeply. In her book, *On Beauty*, Harvard Professor Elaine Scarry describes the experience this way:

> *Not Homer alone but Plato, Aquinas, Plotinus, Pseudo-Dionysius, Dante, and many others repeatedly describe beauty as a "greeting." At the moment one comes into the presence of something beautiful, it greets you. It lifts away from the neutral background as though coming forward to welcome you—as though the object were designed to "fit" your perception.*

Imagine the air "greeting" you, "fainting" from your depth of love.

It does—every time you refresh yourself with an appreciation of beauty. You might see beauty in your own thoughts, in the flash of a diamond on your finger, in the glint and depth in a horse's eye, the laughter of a friend, the selfless act of a stranger.

Originally I had planned for the rose 'New Day' to be my alphabet's *N*. I even photographed an alphabet letter. I changed my mind after passing by a thrilling shrub of 'Nevada' every day for two weeks in Susan Donley's front garden.

Susan entrusted Florali, her flower business, to me while she vacationed in Italy. As I approached her garden studio, 'Nevada' greeted me daily, "baring" all, with wide-open, four-inch almost single flowers of the palest possible pink. A sunny wealth of stamens tint her petals gold near the center, and

'Nevada', moved to another place, is beginning to flourish.

sometimes patches of magenta appear on the petals. Reclining and perching on branches closely padded with light green leaves, her blooms knocked me out. Each flower spoke, "I am beauty, I delight in offering my beauty to creation."

'Nevada' has proved a challenge to grow in our California climate. I've seen flourishing eight-foot shrubs growing in England, but Susan's shrub lost energy and after three years she removed it. I've tried to grow 'Nevada' three times and my new

A 'Nevada' bloom rests in an antique silver saltcellar.

shrub is climbing our fence and finally doing very well. Introduced by Pedro Dot of Spain in 1927, 'Nevada' is carefree and disease-resistant if you can get her established.

AS I APPROACHED THE GARDEN STUDIO, 'NEVADA' GREETED ME DAILY, "BARING" ALL, WITH WIDE-OPEN, FOUR-INCH ALMOST SINGLE FLOWERS OF THE PALEST POSSIBLE PINK.

When my 'Nevada' produces blooms, I'm more than excited and I enjoy a refreshing communion. Intimacy with roses is not helpful to me alone. When you take a moment to let beauty fill your awareness, someone somewhere benefits by the positive energy.

Beauty is such an intriguing subject. One day, in a life-defining moment, I realized that I live a life devoted to beauty. The realization made me feel giddy, whole, and filled with purpose. I realized that I lived to see beauty, to seek beauty, to create beauty, and share beauty. Even though I adore the forms of beauty in creation, I have found that beauty is greater than form. Beauty comes from within. I love that the beauty of roses reveals the beauty within me.

Finding myself delightfully startled at the sight of certain rose images while exploring the Internet one evening, an internal question appeared. Why am I so utterly undone by particular images? Why do I linger over portraits of the Gallica rose named 'Tuscany', revealing her golden cache of stamens in a velvet surround of dark wine-crimson petals, or of 'Lady Forteviot', bowing her head, glittered with dew? Both images, lit by my computer, held me in awe with my mouth open.

Then I remembered other instances: how I gasped at the sight of soaring pink hollyhocks while driving to the transit station. I thought about Mary's cat, Puffin, rubbing her furry white cheeks on my knee; my daughter Anna patting my shoulder. I realized that occurrences that stir me are a mirror of my deeper self. There is a part of me that is as full of meaning and as beautiful as the object or action that captures my attention. I am as kind as the loving gesture I receive and honor. Special moments with beauty are clues to our depth of spirit.

You are as beautiful as the beauty you see, feel, know. Think of the gasps, stirrings, and sighs you experience in your life; they acknowledge the depth of your being. One cultivates self-awareness through receptivity to beauty. Beauty always seeks to energize a person, their loving and their generosity.

'Nevada's' sweeping beauty symbolizes, for me, the depth of my own "glowing breast," my spirit, my heart, my soul. 'Nevada' easily represents the beauty in the fathomless pool of love available to all human beings.

OKLAHOMA

A hand-tied posy of 'Oklahoma' stays put in a slim handblown glass vase.

This chapter is devoted to the rose 'Oklahoma' and a man who was born there, my husband, Leroy Wheeler Parker. His artwork adorns many of these pages, and he's been my partner for thirty-nine years of rose loving.

Leroy and I met in 1964 as students at California College of Arts and Crafts in Oakland. Attractive, smiling Leroy first captured my attention singing blues and playing the guitar on the dorm patio at lunchtime. After we met, we found immediate companionship in our mutual love of art. Married in 1966, we have led a life, with our two daughters, brimming in creative experience. As a family, we held art fairs at our home in the late nineties. Oneita presented fashion designs; Anna sold embroidery; Leroy marketed his art; and I sold greeting cards and photographic prints.

Leroy, a widely exhibited artist, is a master of drawing, painting, sculpture, ceramics, and papermaking. A professor of fine art at San Jose State University, he has inspired students for thirty-two years. He teaches watercolor, life drawing, and a popular course in papermaking that he instituted seventeen years ago. Leroy encourages his students to nurture, create, and prosper with their imaginations.

Leroy loves very dark red roses. In 1999, while I vacationed in Oregon, much

'OKLAHOMA' IS A RARE SPECIMEN, FOR SHE IS ABOUT AS BLACK AS A RED ROSE CAN BE...THE COLOR OF HER RICHLY FRAGRANT BLOOMS REMAINS AS EVEN AS WELL-DYED VELVET.

Fuchsia, strawberry, dahlias, and *R. glauca* leaves and hips join 'Oklahoma' in an Indian brass pot.

to my surprise he transformed the unkempt back corner of our property into his own private rose garden. He designed and planted two rose beds that border a center walkway of cement pavers and bricks. While shopping for roses, Leroy gleefully found his favorite color in the rose named after his home state.

'Oklahoma' is a rare specimen, for she is about as black as a red rose can be. Raised by the American growers Herbert Swim and O.L. Weeks in 1963, the color of her richly fragrant blooms remains as even as well-dyed velvet. When her classic buds unfold, pointed petals curve over each other forming a beguiling center rosette. Allowing a brief pause for admiring her debut, the rosette opens further and the petals change step. They separate and inverse into curling flutes, spreading into an almost perfect globe. Rich bronze-gold anthers lay at the core like a well-set brooch. Her long-stemmed blooms and dark green, leathery leaves are born on a tall, basic Hybrid Tea shrub.

Red roses are often surprisingly sensitive. 'Oklahoma' likes a temperate climate or afternoon shade; during a heat wave, her flowers and leaves will scorch.

I frustrated Leroy for years by asking him not to pick the roses. I wanted them for photo shoots and commercial bouquets. Finally, with his own roses, he is free. He loves to give them away and is happy to let me have as many as I want. On Sundays, Leroy arranges a bouquet to take to his mother, for she too likes red roses in particular. He uses roses for still lifes in his watercolor classes; he

'Oklahoma' in the garden

gives rose bouquets to his art clients; and he makes wonderful big arrangements for art openings. Leroy also likes the rustic, less-than-perfect winter roses and will keep the house beautified with them until the last roses are pruned into dormancy.

Thanks to Leroy's understanding of the creative process, I have been free to pursue all my artistic whims and dreams however impractical or outrageous they seem. From fashion designer, gardener, florist, photographer, and now, writer, Leroy has

One of Leroy's rose drawings on handmade paper imbedded with roses

supported all my aspirations. We have also collaborated on projects. In my fashion business, I made evening gowns out of silk chiffon marbleized by Leroy. I have also made drawings and paintings on his handmade paper, and many sheets are imbedded with rose petals from our garden. My favorite collaboration is my rose arrangements paired with Leroy's imaginative ceramic vessels.

When our garden began to overflow with blooming roses, I experimented with arranging them in Leroy's oversize ceramics, inspired by the large flower arrangements that enthralled me in hotel lobbies, restaurants, and fashion showrooms. What a luxury to learn the art of rose presentation displayed in my husband's artwork! This early experimentation inspired my work in still-life photography.

Leroy and I have very different backgrounds and approaches to life, but somehow we manage to balance our differences. Individually, we are both attuned and eager for the next inspiration. Often our separate interests lead us to new ideas that become part of our collective pool of creativity.

I'm grateful for Leroy's companionship and understanding and to the rose 'Oklahoma' for a gorgeous *O* and the opportunity to present my rose-loving husband.

Leroy in front of his painting *Mega Rose*, part of his one-man show at the Triton Museum in San Jose in 2001. Leroy is a walking work of art—he loves painting his clothes.

PRISTINE

'Pristine', regal yet modest in an abundant basket of roses with *R. multiflora* greens. The arrangement is in a five-gallon plastic bucket.

We planted the rose 'Pristine' outside our front window, hoping for a good show. And we got one. Her performance begins in March. Once 'Pristine's' new, deep-maroon canes and leaves emerge from her thorny, gray winter form, spring progresses daily before our eyes. 'Pristine' dramatizes rose life at every stage. She is the queen and the king of roses.

Queen *and* king? 'Pristine' clearly displays how all roses contain both female (stigma) and male (stamens) characteristics. Her particularly well-defined reproductive organs illustrate why hybridists have enjoyed creating so many new roses—it is relatively easy to make the connection!

Like the rose, each human being has a link between masculine and feminine qualities. My understanding of the link was enlightened one spring when I costumed an opulent fifth-grade production of Shakespeare's *Twelfth Night* at The Meher School across the street.

Max, age 11, played the mischievous and flamboyant Sir Andrew Aguecheek. His straight, blond bangs cut sharply across dark eyebrows inspired a royal concoction of gold and purple velvet. Eye-popping rhinestone buttons, leg-o'-mutton sleeves, puffy bloomers, tights, and a sword finished off his costume.

Max came to his fittings looking droopy in an oversize, gray T-shirt and baggy brown pants. The day he donned his full costume, he smiled and drew himself up proud and tall. His delight in the showy attire brought out the strength and beauty of his masculinity.

'Pristine' caught after dropping her petals

Rose, age 10, always a tomboy, tall, a champion swimmer and basketball player, starred as Lady Olivia. Rose had not worn a dress since she was five years old. She needed two, a black mourning gown and a frivolous party frock. Puffed sleeves, fitted waists, and voluminous petticoats transformed Rose into the elegant young girl she is. She played her part with ease, grace, humor.

The boys appreciated the opportunity to feel free, flashy, and costumed in beauty. The girls shed their T-shirts and jeans and fulfilled princess fantasies. The romance and femininity of sumptuous clothing balanced the masculine qualities in both boys and girls. Like the rose 'Pristine', the children were poised and confident with their dual natures.

Introduced by Bill Warriner of Jackson & Perkins in 1978, 'Pristine' is a high-maintenance rose. The quirks of interbreeding gave 'Pristine' heavenly blooms and horrific thorns. The regal bearing of her long stems and large sculpted blossoms issue from a base of enormous, wide-spreading canes. Huge dark green, leathery leaves outfit the shrub. When grown without hindrance, 'Pristine' has a five- to six-foot diameter. Since my shrub is close to the house, I use reverse pruning to contain her growth. Cutting above a bud-eye that faces the center trains her new growth inward, forming a slimmer shrub.

Her thorns are large, sharp, and thickly studded on every cane. They must be dealt with if you want to arrange her with other flowers. Each thorn must be removed one at a time, with clippers.

My rose garden has one 'Pristine' and I

'Pristine' growing in
Susan Donley's white
garden

wouldn't want any more. One monarch per empire is quite enough! 'Pristine's' quickly evolving blooms are the main reason I love and relish her presence.

If I harvest one stem of 'Pristine' for a bud vase, I leave her thorns intact. The thorns detail her costume, acknowledging the power of her personality. Her chiseled, pink-flushed buds open quickly. Like the palest pink cotton velvet, the enclosing petals become an ample underskirt supporting a layer of immaculate ivory petals. After a spectacular

unfolding, a crown of ruby stamens tipped with rich gold anthers preens in the center.

For three days, 'Pristine' and I commune in deep silence, radiating mutual admiration and love for existence. Then suddenly, all her petals fall into an elaborate heap at the foot of the vase! Sometimes my ears are the first to register this release. I hear petals fall, turn my head to face her, and sigh in acknowledgment. In the dark, laying in bed, I have heard 'Pristine's' petals descend. Her graceful surrender never fails to stir me. Other rose lovers find fault with 'Pristine's' petal drop, but I have learned to look forward to it.

If I could yield to change with 'Pristine's' poise, I'd be the master of myself. I would know that growth and transition pervade every moment of existence.

'Pristine's' forceful (masculine) structure and delicate (feminine) blossoms reflect nature's perfect balance. Connecting with roses like 'Pristine'—or anything truly loved—nurtures balance.

> I HEAR PETALS FALL, TURN MY HEAD TO FACE HER, AND SIGH IN ACKNOWLEDGMENT. HER GRACEFUL SURRENDER NEVER FAILS TO STIR ME.

Above: Her majesty, 'Pristine', in a bud vase, thorns and all **Opposite:** Dreamy 'Pristine' portrait

queen elizabeth

QUEEN ELIZABETH

'Queen Elizabeth' inserted into 'Snowmound' spiraea fills a glass pitcher.

During my childhood, I loved drawing pictures of women. Queen Elizabeth II fascinated me at age seven. I clearly remember her coronation portrait, which appeared on the cover of *Life* magazine in June 1953. I used her image as a reference to draw a bejeweled queen in a splendid gown.

People had been fascinated with England's royalty for several decades. The abdication of King Edward VIII (Elizabeth's uncle) "for the woman he loved," fueled endless news stories. The world kept tabs on his successor and brother, King George VI (Elizabeth's father), who was respected and admired for his activities during and after World War II. He died while Princess Elizabeth was on tour in Africa. The world sympathized, and five months later, at age 27, Elizabeth Alexandra Mary became Queen of England.

In 1954, the world of roses honored the young Queen when Walter Lammerts of

California introduced her namesake. With a flourish of trumpets, the 'Queen Elizabeth' rosebush was an instant success. At first, her remarkable qualities confused American Rose Society officials. The shrub's vigor and size fit none of their categories for modern roses. A new rose class designated Grandiflora was created

IN ENGLAND, HER PINK BLOOMS WAVE ABOVE SMALL GARDEN PLOTS ALL OVER THE COUNTRY, NO DOUBT TO HONOR HER ROYAL NAMESAKE AS WELL TO ENJOY HER FLORAL PERFECTION.

especially for her. To this day, few other roses placed in this class have matched the Queen's stately qualifications. The American classification is not recognized in Britain where 'Queen Elizabeth' is known as a Floribunda.

Essentially an oversize Hybrid Tea, 'Queen Elizabeth' reaches eight feet. She offers a brilliant display of clear bright pink blooms produced in clusters on amaz-

'Limemound' spiraea in floral foam is the base for this charming basket.

ingly long stems. Her leathery, deep green foliage is disease-resistant. It is not surprising that she has received every rose award, including "the world's favorite rose."

In England, I spotted my first 'Queen Elizabeth' rosebush as soon as we reached the streets of London. Her pink blooms wave above small garden plots all over the country, no doubt to honor her royal namesake as well to enjoy her floral perfection. On the short return drive to the airport at the end of our trip, I counted the gardens abloom with this enduring rose—there were thirty-eight!

'Queen Elizabeth' entered our garden as a climber in our first bare root order. We planted her against the chimney. Like Jack's beanstalk, the canes thrust upward with a force of growth I have yet to see duplicated in any other rose. The blooms rambled over the roof, making the house look gorgeous each spring. Contrary to the growing information on the label, the rose barely rebloomed. After four years, the climber lost energy, produced no new canes, and offered only a few spring blooms. After two more years of sparse growth, we sadly removed the rose from our garden.

The shrub of 'Queen Elizabeth' is another story. A noble example has been growing for more than twenty years at The Meher School across the street. 'Queen Elizabeth' roses welcomed both of my daughters to school during their early education. I marvel at her longevity.

Seeing the children holding roses reminds me of an elemental aspect of human nature: Children love to pick flowers and they naturally want to give them to others. Do you remember gathering flowers as a small child? Can you remember your own child offering you a fistful of blooms? We might have forgotten, but we all know how to gather and give flowers.

In pictures of Queen Elizabeth II and in so many of Lady Diana, the women are holding flowers. The English love giving posies to their royalty. They remind me of the bouquets children make.

Susie Kohl, author and teacher at the school, says children are capable of seeing beauty in everything. The two of us often converse about education and our own childhood. We like to consider the effect beauty had on the formation of our consciousness. During one of our discussions, Susie showed me a picture of herself at age four holding a bouquet of wildflowers that she had gathered outside her door.

The children at the school have a strong impact on my gardening. Realizing that they pass our garden daily stimulates my efforts. As a child, I would have loved seeing a beautiful rose garden across from my school. Such an impression can have any number of positive influences.

When I was a little girl, I felt I had no garden, even though I remember rhododendrons planted under my bedroom window, spiraea growing near the garage, and geraniums in a brick planter on the porch. Our backyard seemed empty; there were no plants or trees. With four young children, my parents had little time for gardening. The barren space of scrubby dandelions and brownish clover distressed me. I looked longingly through the fence

In 1990, our 'Queen Elizabeth' climber bloomed at the height of her glory.

slats on all three sides of our yard. In our neighbor's gardens, I saw paths and hedges, raspberries, vegetables, flowers, trees. I wanted all those things in our family's garden. I dug up blue bachelor's buttons from the fields and tried to plant them but they died.

Years later, I realized the empty backyard of my childhood home became a blank canvas for my future. The memories of surrounding gardens were like colorful paints, energizing me as an adult to be free to create and to flourish in unforeseen ways in my own garden.

My alphabet's *Q* evokes another childhood memory, for my maiden name begins with a *Q*—Carolyn Quiett would have loved her initial shaped in 'Queen Elizabeth' roses.

Francesca Cole waiting to give her mother two beribboned stems of 'Queen Elizabeth'

For fifth grade graduation at The Meher School, I arranged these bouquets on my husband's playful sculpture made from tree rounds. 'Philadelphus' and cat-mint help fill the bouquets.

ROULETII

The long thorny canes of 'Rouletii' don't arrange easily, but who could resist trying in this perfectly coordinated Chinese porcelain vase?

I fondly remember the day I purchased this special rose. My journal entry for Sunday, May 21, 1989, describes a heady event:

> Today I treated myself to the Celebration of Old Roses. To my surprise, the annual event and the cottage our family lived in twenty-eight years ago are on the same street in El Cerrito— Ashbury Street—the site of our first rose garden.

> A carnival atmosphere swung me into a throng of Old Rose lovers. Plant vendors lined both sides of the walkway outside the entrance. The delectable roses and perennials tempted me to stop, but I had to see what was going on inside.

At the entryway stood a tall basket that looked like a wicker wedding cake. Packed close together on three tiers were numerous and varied Old Roses in their well-known pinks, mauves, and deep violets.

Walking past raffle tables displaying tempting prizes of superb rosebushes, I tried to contain myself as I entered a scented sea. A rectangle of long tables in the large room displayed a vast assembly of roses. Arranged by family, the roses were all carefully labeled in clear glass bottles. Even though I was by myself in the large crowd, I started laughing—overwhelming beauty had me laughing! I perused the roses, intoxicated by fragrance and splendor. Taking reference notes was useless—I wanted every rose.

Display tables of roses at the Celebration of Old Roses

At the back of the room, artful arrangements of Old Roses waited to be judged. Additional vendors had display tables against the walls. You could purchase a dollop of rose jelly on a cracker, accompanied by a recipe for ten cents; a flower-shaped cookie with rose flavoring for twenty-five cents; china hand-painted with roses; rose clothing; rose greeting cards.

When I was able to tear myself from the room, I walked by the plant vendors again. I purchased two roses I had been looking for, Belinda and Ballerina, and what looked like a darling mini rose labeled 'Rouletii'. I left the memorable event in great happiness.

I planted my three rose purchases in a bed that borders a six-foot redwood fence my husband had recently built. The rose called 'Rouletii' went into the ground next to the opening to the back garden. To my surprise the little mini took off—she climbed the fence! We had to construct a gateway arbor for her. The rose's pale green, twelve-foot canes soon swathed the structure in a tracery of tiny leaves, making an impressive entrance. I like to think that my gardener's intuition planted the rose in such a perfect spot. As a gardener, I've made many planting mistakes; I'm thrilled when nature takes charge and paints her own picture.

As a writer, I might have made another mistake if Graham Thomas hadn't looked at my *R* and said, "That is not 'Rouletii'."

My heart sank as he said, "That's 'Pompon de Paris'; it used to grow in my rock garden. This is going to upset your alphabet isn't it?" Actually, the puzzlement has made my alphabet more interesting.

I tried to solve the identification problem. I have grown a mini rose labeled 'Pompon de Paris' whose flowers look nothing like those on my

THE ROSE'S PALE GREEN, **TWELVE-FOOT CANES SOON SWATHED THE STRUCTURE** IN A TRACERY OF TINY LEAVES, MAKING AN IMPRESSIVE ENTRANCE.

climber. And, a picture that is captioned as 'Rouletii' in Martyn Rix and Roger Phillip's book, *Roses*, looks nothing like the climber either. By chance, I borrowed a book from my friend Mary titled *Gardening With Old Roses* by John Scarman. On page 95, I saw my rose! Labeled 'Pompon de Paris', the photograph shows her familiar perky blooms trimming a building's roof. A picture isn't proof though. I went to a special rose nursery and was informed that rosarians equate the two roses! So, thankfully, I think it's safe to keep the name 'Rouletii' associated with my rose and with the *R* in my alphabet.

On March 19, I picked three of 'Rouletii's' one-and-one-half-inch blooms and set them in water in a Chinese porcelain spoon. Looking at them, I can write a description of magenta buds

'Rouletii' at the gateway to our garden; to the left is 'Yves Piaget'

that open into loose, double petal-puffs of cherry pink. At the center, the petals pale, forming a white bowl that highlights a tiny cluster of yellow stamens. 'Rouletii' or 'Pompon de Paris' are descendants of dwarf China roses and are also the ancestors of modern miniature roses.

Each spring, the media devotes premium space to roses and rose celebrations. Alluring magazine covers alert readers to feature stories extolling roses and rose gardens, and calendars list rose events throughout the world. California is especially fortunate to have many rose celebrations.

The Celebration of Old Roses, where I bought my 'Rouletii', is held at the El Cerrito Community Center the first weekend after Mother's Day and is a labor of love that introduces Old Roses to a wider public. The event is sponsored by The

Above: Miriam Wilkins in her garden **Opposite:** 'Rouletii' in mini vases poses for the author's watercolor painting.

Heritage Roses Group, founded by Miriam Wilkins. The members focus on the preservation, history, reintroduction, and identification of these roses. Miriam lectures frequently, writes the semi-annual *Old Roser's Digest*, and travels, visiting the rose gardens of the world.

Miriam Wilkins' garden has been visited by most of the well-known rosarians in the world. Can you imagine being in a jungle of rare and blissful roses? I've never seen anything like Miriam's garden. It flows eight thousand square feet down a hill and into her neighbor's property. I walked through tunnels of soaring rose canes (Miriam doesn't prune her roses) that looped and braided themselves together to form what looked like a fairy castle. Mesmerized, the question, "What's the name of this rose?" was on the tip of my tongue at every turn. At one point, I was almost buried in a cascade of pale pink singles; a few more paces down the path, I stared into the face of a white rose that took my breath away. It seems like Miriam grows every rose in existence.

The journal entry at the beginning of the chapter traced my early learning about rose gardening to our cottage on Ashbury Street, very near Miriam's home and only two blocks away from the El Cerrito center. I knew nothing about Miriam and her Celebration of Old Roses at that time, but in retrospect, I believe their proximity had a magical influence on my rose future.

'Rouletii' inspired me to make my first alphabet letter. If I hadn't associated 'Rouletii' with the initial *R* there might not have been a rose alphabet.

Opposite page, left to right: 'Rouletii 'in an egg cup; 'Rouletii' posy in a small vase **This page, left to right:** 'Rouletii' in a porcelain spoon; 'Rouletii' in one of my mother's demitasse cups

SWEET SURRENDER

Crossed stems of 'Annabelle' hydrangea form the base for an insertion of 'Sweet Surrender' and 'Florida Plena' clematis.

In 1985, during our first spring at Meek Place, Leroy came home with two unusual packages: short, naked rose canes fringed the top of puffy, plastic-wrapped cylinders. Labeled 'Apricot Nectar' and 'Sweet Surrender', they were our first store-bought roses. With a mix of curiosity, excitement, and nervousness, I tried to figure out how to care for my husband's gift. I had never planted a bare root rose. I didn't want to make mistakes with what appeared to be fragile plants. I carefully read the directions on the wrapping and planted the two roses in the front bed.

Then began a process I became addicted to: watching and waiting for roses to bloom for the first time. They did not disappoint. 'Sweet Surrender's' blooms wowed me. I couldn't believe my good fortune. Her petals, like ruffles and folds of shimmering pink silk, peak at each stage of unfolding as her stamens remain artfully concealed. Slightly unfurled or fully open, she looks divine pinned to a blazer or a ball gown. The potency of her fragrance almost embarrasses me. I feel I'm intruding on the union of heady perfume and deep musk.

Introduced in California by O.L. Weeks in 1983, the 'Sweet Surrender' shrub

'SWEET SURRENDER' IS A STAR. A REAL FOCAL POINT IN A BOUQUET. SHE BRINGS EVERYONE'S EYES RIGHT TO HER.

has the leggy, stiff, and upright characteristics of a Hybrid Tea. For the past two years, my shrub seems to have lost its vitality, and because I couldn't imagine my garden without her, I tried to find another. Since the market is deluged with new Hybrid Teas every year, 'Sweet Surrender' wasn't easy to locate. I tried several places without results. Then I remembered Regans, the large rose nursery and mail-order business in Fremont, California. I called in the summer, and they told me they would have 'Sweet Surrender' in stock the next fall. What a relief! Regans

'Sweet Surrender' afloat in handblown glass

carries 1,100 different roses. It's fascinating to buy them bare root at this nursery. The roses don't come in tight plastic bundles with half their roots chopped off. They are categorized alphabetically and buried into compost in large raised beds.

'Sweet Surrender's' open blooms are fairly flat and, because they sometimes have a weak neck, the flowers may droop in an arrangement. But by all means, don't let that stop you! 'Sweet Surrender' is a star, a real focal point in a bouquet. She brings everyone's eyes right to her. Her great beauty and her compelling name beg me to tell you two tales of surrender.

First, during an early phase of our gardening, I received a phone call from a woman named Claire, who said, "Carolyn, do you mind if I come and walk in your garden from time to time?"

I replied, "Not at all, please do."

I was touched and surprised that she would want to spend time in our unfinished garden. While visiting one day, Claire said, "Your garden reminds me of

'Sweet Surrender' in a silver flute with *R. roxburghii* leaves

my favorite place on earth." She recalled a verdant paradise of roses and exotic plants she had visited in India.

Claire had a rare and debilitating disease that she battled for many years. In the later stages, she had to give up her home and garden, because her husband left her. Eventually, she was only able to see her teenage daughter on occasion.

After moving from her home, Claire called and asked if I would like to have her potted rosebushes. I

'Sweet Surrender' wrapped in floral tape and pinned to a linen blazer

Claire entered my life like a rose in full bloom. Maybe she intuited her imminent parting from this life and needed the nurturance of a vibrant garden. I had the privilege of her acquaintance while she prepared her surrender.

A different account of giving oneself up begins with a poem Theophile Gautier wrote about a rose like 'Sweet Surrender'.

THE SPECTER OF THE ROSE

I am the spirit of a rose
You wore yesterday to the ball.
You took me from the garden
Still covered with the pearls
Of silver tears
And among the star-strewn crowd
All night you danced with me.
What admirable destiny was mine
To have so beautiful a death
More than one would have given his life,
For I had your bosom for my tomb
And on the alabaster where I rest
A poet has written with a kiss:
Here lies a rose
Which kings would die, if they could be

THEOPHILE GAUTIER 1811–1872
TRANSLATED BY RICHARD DEANE

told her I'd love to have them. When Leroy and I drove over to pick them up, Claire invited us into her new apartment. The spotless, almost empty space looked and felt like the interior of a luminous shell.

The next time I heard from Claire was the day she found a lifeless female dove, still warm, with its wings spread out on her doorstep. When she knelt down to pick up the dove, she heard its mate chirp a farewell. She asked me if she could bury the dove in our garden. We buried the velvety gray dove, wrapped in newspaper, in the moist earth under 'Sweet Surrender'. Four months later, Claire died.

In 1911, Gautier's poem inspired Michel Fokine to choreograph a ballet for Vaslav Nijinsky. Regarded as the greatest male dancer of the twentieth century, Nijinsky was born in Russia in 1890. His parents were both dancers. Dancing was like breathing to Vaslav. He felt agitated even as a small boy if he could not practice. After spending his first ten years touring and dancing with his parents, he became a student at the Imperial Ballet School in St. Petersburg. His abilities awed his teachers, and he quickly matured with perfect technique. He could leap with acrobatic ease to great heights and, for a moment, suspend himself in the air. During his ten-year career, he was renowned for becoming the essence of his characters: faun, slave, god, clown, spring, wind, fragrance. With lightness and softness he entered a different dimension while dancing.

Nijinsky danced *Le Spectre de la Rose* with Tamara Karsavina in Paris for the Ballets Russes. Before each performance, pink and lilac rose petals were sewn to his tights. A cap of the same silky petals covered his hair. As the soul of roses, he leapt through a window to reunite with the slumbering maiden. Vera Krasovskaya in her biography, *Nijinsky*, writes: "In a dreamy atmosphere they swirled and waltzed: she in the allusiveness of her pauses and poses, he in the delicate chiaroscuro of his movements, weightless, elusive, embodying the perfume possessed by the Spirit of the Rose."

Nijinsky surrendered to nature and nature held him afloat. Surrender finely tunes every art form and shapes life's moments, both simple and profound. 'Sweet Surrender's' exquisite name and beauty give form to nature's symbols and gifts.

Nijinsky dressed in rose petals for *Spectre de la Rose*

TRADESCANT

Susan, who is a florist, arranged 'Tradescant' in a metal urn with monochromatic flowers from her garden. She began with a base of floral foam.

After many years of gardening and a lifelong fascination with plants and color, my friend, Susan Donley, began creating her dream garden. The rose 'Tradescant' glows in her black-plum border as one of the notes in Susan's meticulous orchestration of color themes. Susan has always gardened—I met her during her pink and white phase. She encouraged my interest in roses.

In 1998, when Susan and her husband, Tim, moved into their home on a hillside facing Mt. Diablo in California, she had a vision of how she wanted her garden to be. Her dream combined her years of gardening experience with a life-defining trip to England in 1991. At Sissinghurst and Hadspen House, Susan saw entire garden rooms devoted to single color schemes. The impressions of Vita Sackville-West's white garden at Sissinghurst and the color theme gardens at Hadspen percolated in Susan's consciousness for seven years.

At their new property, Susan and Tim removed every plant and tree except for a bountiful Meyer lemon. This dab of yellow, the only limitation on Susan's blank canvas, inspired a welcoming bed of sunny color to greet visitors as they enter the back garden. A striking combination of yellow roses, 'Graham Thomas', 'Golden Celebration', 'Maréchal Niel', 'Golden Wings', 'The Pilgrim', and 'Lady Banks',

'TRADESCANT' IS AN ENGLISH ROSE DESCRIBED AS HAVING A REFRESHINGLY SHARP DAMASK FRAGRANCE. THE DARK CLARET-CRIMSON BLOOMS, PACKED WITH PETALS, JOIN PRETTY ROUND BUDS ON LONG STEMS.

join witch hazel, yellow dogwood, foxglove, native iris, and columbine. Yellow pansies with hints of peach lead the eye across a peach sandstone terrace to a bed at the back of the house bordered by peachy pink pansies and 'Iceland' poppies.

An equally impressive combination of peach roses—'Just Joey', 'Evelyn', 'Apricot Nectar', 'Tamora', 'Sweet Juliet', 'Sally Holmes', 'Penelope', and 'Cressida' planted with 'Café Ole' and 'Baby Girl' dahlias—echoes the peach tones of the sun rising over Mt. Diablo. The eight-feet-deep bed of

'Tradescant' floats with candles and 'Angel Face' roses.

'Tradescant' growing in
Susan's front border

layered plantings becomes soft pink as it continues around the side of the garden and melds at the back into lavenders and blues. A climactic rush of electric blue from perennial morning glories climbing the back fence completes the picture. All this bor-

ders an oval patch of lawn where an 'Iceberg' rose climbing an old apricot tree presides over Susan's panoramic scheme.

In the front garden, Susan plays with white. Silver-green foliage plants combined with white

perennials add texture to a most intoxicating assembly of white roses.

In a narrow bed on the flip side of the white garden, separated by a fence next to the street, 'Tradescant' is nestled in an absorbing collection of monochromatic plant material. Black hollyhocks, pansies, and poppies, 'Queen of the Night' irises, maroon akebia, 'Ruby Glow' loropetalum, and clematis viticella grow with 'Violette', 'News', and 'Tuscany Superb' roses.

'Tradescant' is an English Rose introduced by David Austin in 1993 and described as having a refreshingly sharp Damask fragrance. The dark claret-crimson blooms, packed with petals, join pretty round buds on long stems, making it ideal for arranging. Bright green, shapely leaves shine on a lanky four-by-five-foot shrub that tends to have an open, spreading center.

Above: 'Tradescant' on an embroidered silk napkin welcomes a dinner guest. **Opposite:** In Susan's white garden, R. mulliganii covers the arch; the other roses are 'Snowbird', 'Marie Pavié', 'Sally Holmes', 'Sombreuil', 'Winchester Cathedral', 'Mme Hardy', and 'Windrush'.

Susan's gardening approach mystified me at first. I preferred a subtle mix of colors that play off of each other with occasional bright colors. I used to think Susan's style was limited. On the contrary, I came to realize her immersion in monochromatic color gives her a structure for free expression. Her plant choices develop from her meditation within diversity. Careful research and intense curiosity reward her with an abundance of varied and appropriate plants for each color theme.

When I finally had a chance to see the gardens in England that inspired her, like Susan, my gardening conceptions turned upside down. At Sissinghurst, it was a joy to be in Vita Sackville-West's White Garden after reading about it for so many years. Vita was a great plants woman. In one of her newspaper columns, she wrote that she uses plants "with careful selection and definite intention." In the garden, a central pergola draped with white *Rosa mulliganii* is flanked by beds bordered in boxwood that contain a wealth of white flowers, flowering shrubs, and silver foliage plants. White delphinium, campanula, foxglove, gypsophilia, Chinese bellflower, white cistus, white hydrangea, white tree peony, and many others create a soothing yet dramatic ambiance.

Hadspen is the eighteenth-century home belonging to the family of garden designer Penelope Hobhouse. In 1987, Canadian designers Nori and Sandra Pope brought their refined knowledge of plants and their interest in color theme gardening to Hadspen. In their book, *Color by Design*, they write, "Whenever possible we strive to move

from light to dark, short to tall, pale to saturated, with the monochrome rhythm driving the composition forward."

The warmth of an old brick wall that once enclosed a kitchen garden inspired the warm tones of the Curved Border. Beginning with yellow, the colors continue on through orange, red, plum, pink, peach, and end in another bed of yellow. A walk along this brilliant planting is a horticultural and artistic education. In the orange section, the lime green leaves of orange nasturtiums climb the wall as the almost black leaves of burnt orange dahlias make a show in front of them. Spikes of flaming crocosmia and bronze phormium offer a striking textural change as they intensify the flaring scheme. On a cooler note, the Peach Walk above the Lily Pond soothed us in shades of lavender, pink, and white. Susan and I lingered in the garden at Hadspen and even went a second time to learn from the absorbing plant and color combinations.

Plant searches are a way of life for Susan and me. Thankfully, specialty nurseries abound in our part of the world. Very close to home is a plant lover's paradise named Moraga Garden Center run by second-generation nurseryman Ken Murakami. Almost weekly during the early days of my garden, I spent time at Ken's studying, gleaning, and filling my car with precious plants. Ken's mind is a storehouse of horticultural knowledge. I love to ask him my burning questions.

While at Sissinghurst two years ago, a particular grass with a white puffy flower intrigued Susan. On the spot, she wrote a postcard to Ken asking if he could obtain the plant. He ordered seeds and is now offering the grass for sale.

Thank goodness for intrepid plantsmen! My alphabet's *T* was named after two of them, the John Tradescants, a seventheenth-century father-son duo. The December 2000 issue of the gorgeous British magazine *Gardens Illustrated* features a profile of the biography, *The John Tradescants* by Prudence Leith-Ross. Here's a short passage: "Father and son were gardeners to a king and kings among gardeners. They were exceptional men, brave inquisitive travelers, seekers after scientific truth, and creators and curators of the first natural history museum in Britain open to the public."

The Tradescants were among an illustrious group of plant seekers who traveled the world from the seventeenth to the nineteenth centuries searching for exotic delights to grow in Britain's temperate climate. We have all benefited from the treasures they discovered. Two historical novels about the Tradescants by Phillipa Gregory, *Earthly Joys* and *Virgin Earth*, offer more fascinating insights into the plant hunter's world.

Planted artfully in the garden of a dear friend, 'Tradescant' immersed me in Susan's view of color harmony, thereby adding a new dimension to life, creativity, and this alphabet.

I crossed the stems of 'Tradescant' as they went into this arrangement to keep them in place in the wide mouth of this mercury glass cube.

unknown

UNKNOWN

'Redcoat' in an opulent setting with 'Graham Thomas', 'Oklahoma', *R. spinosissima* greens, and yellow abutilon blooms

In my garden, three roses represent Unknown, a frustrating rose world category. I don't remember if the open-faced red beauty ever had a nametag—if she did, I lost it. The pink and yellow roses were in our backyard when we moved here.

I can't think of anyone I know who hasn't lost the name of a rose or moved to a property with unlabeled roses.

Will Tillotson, founder of Roses of Yesterday and Today (pages 89-92), used the category to his advantage by offering his customers grab bag sales of unblooming roses that had lost their labels.

At the Celebration of Old Roses (mentioned on pages 127-128), people are invited to bring roses they want to identify. On a special display table labeled "Unknown Roses," note cards and pencils are provided for answers and guesses.

Unknown also refers to *foundlings*. From 1870 to 1970, cemeteries across America and gardens in the South were flourishing with sophisticated Old Roses that had lost their names. Thankfully, the waves of change and fashion in the rose world had stopped at the graveyard. Thomas Christopher writes in his book, *In Search of Lost Roses*: "…for whereas each generation is apt to relandscape the gar-

SINCE THE RED ROSE IS THE MOST OUTSTANDING OF MY GARDEN'S THREE UNKNOWNS, I REALLY WANTED TO LAUD HER CHARMS, BUT HOW COULD I WHEN HER NAMELESS- NESS RENDERED HER UNAVAILABLE?

A posy in an apple juice jar that I photographed before giving to my friend Jim

den, few of us would root up the rose that was planted by grandmother's grave."

Christopher talks about "rose rustlers," gardeners who rescued America's Old Roses. He mentions Carl Cato in Lynchburg, Virginia:

> *He found especially good hunting in the older black neighborhoods. Around the weather-beaten frame houses and sagging verandas he'd find glorious blossoms—later, with catalogs and handbooks he'd identify these as roses of the most distinguished European descent. Few of the owners he interviewed knew what they had, though many had a lively appreciation of the flowers. It is Carl's belief that the roses found their way into those neighborhoods generations ago as cuttings that black gardeners took in their white employers' gardens. It is testimony to the black gardeners' taste that they kept the roses long after their employers succumbed to the itch for novelty.*

Christopher tells the story of a woman named Pamela Puryear who saw her first Old Rose in 1969. She found a huge specimen of the China Rose 'Old Blush' flourishing next to an abandoned log cabin in rural Texas. Pamela was astounded that the neglected rose had survived many years of Texas heat and drought. Since her Hybrid Teas always died in the harsh climate, she thought about replacing them with this more hardy type.

She began searching out and collecting cuttings of old abandoned roses and found that they

'Redcoat' in full bloom

flourished in her garden. Soon, other enthusiastic gardeners joined her searches. They would all set off together on a rural tour, stopping at cemeteries and the overgrown yards of abandoned homes. Before taking cuttings, they'd do what they could to ensure the rose's survival by trimming away dead wood and removing competing weeds.

Old homes with mature gardens were also a boon to their collecting. They'd make acquaintance with the owners who were almost always happy to

share the rose riches that had been in their gardens and neighborhoods for years.

Mike Shoup, a Texas nurseryman, joined the group. In two years, Mike assembled cuttings of three hundred different rose cultivars! They became the parent plants of a nursery and mail-order business he named The Antique Rose Emporium.

With the help of rose rustlers, lovers, and purveyors across the country, America's Old Roses are no longer unknown. In the past thirty years, they have been identified or given study names until their true identity can be established.

Many Unknowns still don't have their original names, but most have been researched and listed. Almost all the roses are available through mail-order catalogs.

Since the red rose is the most outstanding of my garden's three Unknowns, I really wanted to laud her charms, but how could I when her namelessness rendered her unavailable? To my surprise,

'Redcoat' with 'Old Master', 'Double Delight', and 'White Masterpiece'

I found her identity in England without even looking!

'Redcoat' introduced herself to me in one of the garden rooms at David Austin's nursery. She is a very fragrant English Rose introduced in 1973. The quickly reblooming, disease-resistant shrub has unique and decorative appeal in the garden and in rose arranging.

I thought about the "unknown" in the creative process as I wrote about Unknown roses. Roses seem to nudge me to look beyond the garden bed for symbols and metaphors. For example, 'Sweet Surrender' made me think of Nijinsky's surrender to nature as he twirled and leaped.

Even though I had thought about what I wanted to say before I began writing this chapter, fear of the unknown gripped me more than it usually does. In a state of mild unrest one morning, I walked into my husband's studio and saw a new painting lying on the floor. Bright colors in abstract shapes and washes were the background for a sentence of four-inch letters painted in white that spelled out, "I love the unknown!"

When I told a writer friend about this incident, she laughed saying, "The unknown is after you, Carolyn."

I remembered *The Artist's Way*, Julia Cameron's book about unblocking creativity. I found the book and opened it three times, stopping when I found this quote by Claude Bernard: "Man can learn nothing except by going from the known to the unknown."

Like you, I have stepped into the unknown

My pink Unknown rose

My yellow Unknown rose

'Redcoat' and 'Chevy Chase' in a Chinese vase

every day of my life. By the unknown, I mean that I never know the outcome of my day or the end result of creativity.

Even though I've made hundreds of big flower arrangements, I always pass through a little fear of the unknown. After all, an empty vase is like a void. With my idea and materials at hand, I start working with the flowers. Soon after I begin, I often think "Eek, what comes next? Is this really going to work?" Then I join my inner familiarity with nature and beauty and the arrangement turns out better than I had hoped. The process is often magical and surprising.

Each art I have pursued, I loved first. I loved photography with all my heart, but fear of the unknown made me think, *Oh, I could never do that.* Then I did it! I was swept away by the poetry while researching for *The Poetry of Roses* and again thought, *Oh, I could never write.* But my experience with roses created a path that gave me no choice. I had to learn to write.

Each of us has a love for particular aspects of creation. Nurturing that love invariably leads to the unknown. Rewarding experience and knowledge always fol-

low. The unknown might be uncomfortable, but once the door is open, it becomes familiar and yields more than I ever thought possible.

I opened a door to the unknown when I began this book. Now that it is almost finished, I find that as I work out the details, information voluntarily turns up to correct mistakes or add interest. Even though I am very familiar with the roses in my alphabet, the facts surrounding their history are often confusing and require researching many sources.

Just this morning, I was searching on the Internet to purchase *Roses*, an out-of-print book. The author, Jack Harkness, was a respected British rose hybridist and writer who I have not yet researched. The book was unavailable.

An hour later, I was handed a copy of *Roses*! I happened to have an appointment with Bob Cowden, the founder of the rose garden at The Gardens at Heather Farm in Walnut Creek. *Roses* sits on a shelf in the library there. Bob knew Will Tillotson and told me about his grab bag sales of roses without labels.

Entering the unknown I've found answers, information, and inspiration well beyond the scope of my hopes and dreams, even the name of my alphabet's *U*!

'Redcoat' hand-gathered in both small and medium arrangements

VIOLETTE

Hand-tied 'Violette' stems stay anchored in the globe.

People always ask me, "Where do you get your roses?" I tell them that I acquire roses from several sources. Then I let them know that my favorite resource is Vintage Gardens in Sebastopol, California.

When I needed examples of roses that weren't already in my garden, for *K, V,* and *Z,* I knew Vintage Gardens would have what I wanted. Although the nursery is sixty-five miles from my home, I make several trips a year. I always go with a gardening friend and sometimes with a whole car full of gardeners.

Located in the country on the Old Gravenstein Highway in Sonoma County, Vintage Gardens sells the world's largest collection of roses. I usually have a list of roses I want when I go to this nursery. I also look forward to being tempted by roses that catch my fancy in the dazzling array collected by the owners, Gregg Lowery and Phillip Robinson.

Over 2,650 varieties of roses are listed in the *Vintage Gardens Complete Catalogue of Antique & Extraordinary Roses.* They also have an extensive online catalog with pictures. Most of my alphabet's roses are offered at Vintage Gardens. Not all varieties listed are available at any given time. It is possible, however, to custom-order all the roses. People are encouraged to fulfill their wildest rose-growing dreams. It takes eighteen months to two years to provide custom-rooted plants, for almost all of the roses at Vintage Gardens are grown on their own roots,

I CHOSE 'VIOLETTE' FROM THE VINTAGE CATALOG INDEX—SHE SOUNDED LIKE A FRENCH CHARMER.

It was a delight to use my favorite demitasse cup for this picture.

a feature I especially welcome. In the catalog Gregg Lowery writes:

> *Own-root plants are never troubled with suckering from rootstocks, and as a result settle into the garden for a lifetime of enjoyment. Often the lifetime of an own-root rose will exceed that of the gardener; so that like a tree it may become the lasting legacy of one gardener.*

The Vintage Gardens catalog is an invaluable resource work. It lists and describes, both historically and horticulturally, fifty-one classes of roses. Charming diagrams clearly illustrate the scale and growth habit of all the roses. There are articles on rose preservation, information about Old Roses, recommended organizations, and an extensive bibliography. Lowery and Robinson have even compiled a wonderful time line called "200 Years of Roses" with a rose introduction listed for each year. You can commemorate a birth or anniversary with a rose—in 1800, the rose 'Duchess of Portland' was introduced; in 1946, 'Lilac Dawn'; in 2000 'Cosmo' came on the scene.

Lowery and Robinson grow all the 2,650 roses listed and more in their own garden. Living with the roses, they are able to personally document growth habit and attributes for the catalog's descriptions. They also host a popular open garden. In 2001, they advertised:

> *Get ready for our annual Open Garden, when our home garden of 3,400 roses opens each weekend in May. We have finally planted our new*

I enjoy weaving 'Violette' canes through our 2'x2' lattice deer fence.

section of old Hybrid Teas and Floribundas, some 900 plants, and it promises to be the most spectacular year yet.

I chose 'Violette' from the Vintage Gardens catalog index—she sounded like a French charmer. Her one-inch blooms, whose stamens look like gold coins in burgundy velvet-lined pouches, grow in clusters amongst shiny leaves. 'Violette' is a twelve- to fourteen-foot Rambler raised by the

Frenchman Turbat in 1921. Ramblers bloom only once and produce flowers on the previous season's canes.

In the Vintage Gardens catalog section on Ramblers, Lowery says a style trend in the early 1900s "fueled a mania for new (old-fashioned) ramblers whose lax and flexible growth was fancifully wrapped on pillars, pergolas, and elaborate trelliage."

'Violette' didn't grow much the first year; I barely had enough flowers to make an arrangement. But after blooming, a sturdy shoot appeared in the middle of the shrub and was soon followed by ten others that were even longer! Since there were so many new shoots, I cut away most of the canes that had flowered and wove the new canes through our fence. They were supple and easy to work with. Even though 'Violette' is on the outside and sometimes gets nipped, her wealth of canes makes up for minor losses.

Ramblers are prostrate unless given support. They are great ground covers for a hillside and can be trained to grow high into trees. Ramblers are very hardy and often evergreen in Zones 8-10.

In a catalog section titled "Provenance," Gregg Lowery thanks all the people, rose businesses, and institutions that have contributed roses to his and Robinson's remarkable collection. This brings the word *volunteer* to my mind. So far in this chapter, *V* is the initial for a rose, and a rose nursery. I'd also like *V* to stand for *volunteer*, a word with a marvelous twofold connotation in the world of gardening. The first is for people; the second is for plants.

Trained on a metal pillar at Nymans in England, 'Violette' shows how flexible she is.

Countless people have voluntarily aided in the preservation of roses created throughout history: the first human being who dug up a rosebush from the wild and planted it near her hut, the monks who filled their monastery courtyards with wild roses, the plant hunters like the Tradescants, collectors like Empress Josephine, rose rustlers in Texas, Miriam Wilkins and The Heritage Roses Group. Then there are those who volunteer their time and energy at public rose gardens and events, and anyone like you or me who have dug up canes or offered cuttings to another rose seeker.

Secondly, there are the naturally occurring volunteers that are a constant delight in the garden. I only have space here to mention the volunteers in the rose kingdom. My alphabet includes at least six sports. Then there are all the pollen-crossings that resulted in new rose breeds. These exchanges took place by chance once people started planting different rose species together. Rose history begins with species roses followed by volunteers!

Verily, *V* proves to be a vehicle for praise in my alphabet. The rose 'Violette', the nursery Vintage Gardens, and the volunteer people and plants of the world deserve vast appreciation!

VOLUNTEERS

For more on the volunteers mentioned here, refer to the following pages: pages 96-99 (Empress Josephine), page 130 (Miriam Wilkins and The Heritage Roses Group), page 146 (Tradescants), and pages 150-152 (rose rustlers).

'Violette' is the filler for an insertion of 'Prospero' and 'The Squire' roses in my husband Leroy's vase.

white masterpiece

WHITE MASTERPIECE

The fragility of this Venetian glass vase required careful arranging. Cream California poppies, white nigella and columbine, 'Snowmound' spiraea, feverfew, and 'Macrantha' roses are inserted with 'White Masterpiece' into a base of 'Silversheen' pittosporum.

'White Masterpiece' joined the garden with seven other white roses on a cool, sunny autumn afternoon. My impulsive purchase was a sheer sign of infatuation. That was seventeen years ago and the luster of white roses continues to woo me. The regal demeanor of 'White Masterpiece' made her an easy choice for my alphabet's *W*.

I imagine that the first rose in creation, over thirty-five million years ago, was white or white with a blush of pink. A mere 2,300 years ago, Homer, in the *Iliad*, was the first to mention the word rose in reference to perfume used by Aphrodite. Legends followed—in one story, white roses blew over the sea after the birth of Aphrodite. White roses became red when she accidentally fell into a thicket while rescuing Adonis—her bleeding wounds colored the roses. In literature, roses spring from the tears and blood of gods, saints, and heroes.

In the garden one morning, I unknowingly brushed against a rose thorn and didn't realize I was wounded until I saw my blood on the petal of a white rose. Startled, I thought, "How beautiful." For a moment, I was living in a poem—only the rose and I knew the lines.

Tradition says that the prophet Mohammed was a man of such beauty and love, his palms smelled of roses. A white rose became visible through Mohammed's sweat, and so roses existed as a sacred flower in Arabia. Fallen petals were protected from being trod upon.

White roses reflect many colors. Green, yellow, pink, peach, lavender, and blue join the vast range of tints captured in the iridescent cells on their petals. Dewdrops caught in the light become diamonds and pearls on white roses. The

IN THE GARDEN, WHEN I KNOW 'WHITE MASTERPIECE' IS BLOOMING, I OFTEN SLOW MY PACE AS I APPROACH SO I CAN FOCUS ON A SPIRALING BUD. THE POISE AND GRANDEUR OF THIS ROSE INSPIRES MOMENTS OF SILENCE.

sun finds its own image in the golden stamens of single white roses.

Because white roses only reflect color, they have a stately, sculptural persona; their form stands out to be studied and admired. Their regal qualities idealize and represent the entire genus *Rosa*.

In white roses, poets and rose lovers see faces with an intimate narrative. They are the spirit of love and purity. Bring a white rose to your own face, breathe in beauty, and know yourself. In the following poem, Rainer Maria Rilke shares this deep rose intimacy.

Rose, I'm so aware of your every part
that our beings are fused.
In this embrace you are confused
with my celebrating heart.

I breathe you in, rose,
as if you were life's whole.
In this one breath I know
a perfect friend, soul to soul.

FROM LES ROSES
TRANSLATED BY RACHEL DACUS

Rilke doesn't say his rose is white, but it's easy to imagine his muse could be any of the white roses described here.

'White Masterpiece' was introduced in 1969 by Eugene Boerner. Her parents were two unnamed seedlings. In my garden, the shrub measures three feet by four feet. The blooms are standouts, with thick, sturdy, ruffled petals that look like wings about to fly. Brushstrokes of green line the center of the outer petals and are a charming accessory to the green glow at the heart of the flowers. However, the blooms are quite heavy and tend to weigh down the stems.

In the garden, when I know 'White Masterpiece' is blooming, I often slow my pace as I approach so I can focus on a spiraling bud. The poise and grandeur of this rose inspire moments of silence and communion. Her fragrance is a rich perfume.

Another white rose, 'Evening Star' came as a gift during my fashion design days. A generous friend and employee, Ronnie Deitrick, planted the fragrant shrub by the entrance of our first design studio. She transformed a patch of scrubby dirt into a welcoming sight.

I watched 'Evening Star' closely. With an inner

Ample rainfall in the winter of 2005 made for spectacular blooms.

yellow tint, her petals unfolded like fabric. She reminded me of the ivory velvet and the cream silk charmeuse on the shelves in our studio. Bending down to take in her delicious scent, for a moment, I'd keep my cheek close to her petals. After closing the studio at that site, I moved 'Evening Star' home to our front garden.

One autumn, I experienced a special rapport with an 'Evening Star' bloom. On my way for a morning walk, I stopped for a whiff from a newly opened flower. In the cool, crisp morning, her heady scent seemed to spring from an eternal pool. The flower lasted for days and was going to remain a vessel of fragrance whether or not anyone inhaled it. This stunned me and made me realize, yet again, how roses, once they are blooming, unconditionally offer their beauty to God and his universe.

The white rose 'Snowbird' grew in our first rose garden. Twenty-five years ago, Leroy took cuttings and propagated her when we moved. I discovered her identity only recently when I saw her in bloom at Vintage Gardens nursery. I was thrilled to see this gem of a rose back in commerce and purchased two more. The first three petals on her elegant, round buds interlock into a frilled propeller before they unfurl into flat mandalas holding over a hundred pure white, perfectly placed petals. Ecstatically fragrant, this wonderful shrub is always trim and well behaved. A Hybrid Tea with an old-fashioned look, she does well growing in large pots.

'Macrantha', found in France in 1823, is another one of my prize spring bloomers. When I first saw her generous supply of bright yellow stamens, she endeared herself to me for life. I love to see this rose in the early morning before the bees have made a

From left to right: 'Macrantha'; 'Snowbird'; 'Mme Hardy'; 'Evening Star'

thousand trips to collect pollen. The buds open into five heart-shape petals of palest pink and close white at the end of the day. They are the embodiment of the roses Botticelli showered on Venus in his famous painting. I enjoy placing ready-to-open 'Macrantha' buds in a bouquet of white roses. When they unfurl their simplicity adds freshness and flair.

'Mme Hardy', the famous white Damask, is unrivaled. Graham Thomas calls her "sumptuous and ravishing." Decorative, leafy sepals pull back from rose-tinted buds. Pure white petals unfurl ruffled and tucked around a mint green button eye. There's

an innocence about this rose that has no descriptive words. Sighs will suffice. In an English churchyard, as Susan and I walked around ancient graves, we both sighed and exclaimed as we came upon this adorable rose blooming unattended with quiet dignity.

White roses are like a bridge between heaven and earth. Their fragrance and beauty seems to transcend time and space. Thanks to *W*, I can share treasured moments with these fair beings.

ROSA MULTIFLORA
ALIAS MADAME X

A few blooms of 'Madame X' spill from a mini birdbath sitting on a bed of isotoma.

In the spring of 1989, three months after the closing of my fashion design business, my friend Mary invited me on a garden outing that had a pivotal impact on my future. We went to the Flower Show at Filoli, near Woodside, California. That day, I became aware of the many possibilities my garden could offer me. I also purchased a petite white single rose in a gallon can labeled 'Madame X'.

William Bourn II built the 654-acre Filoli estate in 1917. Bourn's wealth came from a gold mine and investments in California's land and water resources. After Bourn died, the William P. Roth family purchased Filoli. The garden gained worldwide recognition in the Roth's care. In 1975, Mrs. Roth donated 125 acres, which includes the manor and gardens, to the National Trust for Historic Preservation.

Local flower arrangers are given the opportunity to show their skills at Filoli's annual spring open house. Floral displays complement the magnificent rooms of the brick mansion. In the ballroom, a glorious floral concoction set on a marble pillar held me in rapture. With great style and feeling, someone had gathered an eclectic mix of plant material. Unusual perennials peeked through masses of many

'MADAME X' SEEMED RATHER WELL BEHAVED TOO, FOR WITHOUT ANY TRAINING, SHE FORMED A FLAT WALL OF SHINY GROWTH.

different Old Roses, cuttings from flowering shrubs gave structure, and blooming vines curled and trailed through the presentation. I carefully studied the bouquet's

A French pastis glass holds hips and blooms.

details and its form. A window on my future seemed to open and I internally vowed to grow a garden that would provide endless possibilities for presenting roses.

After luxuriating in the arrangements, my friend and I toured Filoli's extensive gardens. I took note of the pruning techniques on 'Gold of Ophir' roses climbing one of the brick walls. Mary and I both marveled at the garden's many features: wisteria draping a row of towering yews, a knot garden of carefully pruned herbaceous plants, a forest of camellias, an impressive beech hedge, and extensive perennial borders. Even though Filoli's gardens are formal and grand, I received numerous ideas for my own small garden.

I planted 'Madame X' at the midpoint of a new fence. She surprised me by quickly covering the fence's fourteen-foot span. She seemed rather well behaved too, for without any training, she formed a flat wall of shiny growth. Since I am so fond of singles, I enjoyed having this energetic new variety. Blooming in clusters, fully open flowers join buds that resemble tiny pearls. After blooming, bunches of miniature, green, berrylike hips turn a decorative red. Late in summer, more blooms mingle with the hips in a handsome textural display.

When I lauded 'Madame X's' characteristics to Karen Talbot, a friend and knowledgeable rosarian, she doubted the rose's name. For a while she thought it might be an unrecorded rose and toyed with naming it 'Carolyn's Climber'—after me! When she saw an exact likeness of the rose as a three-foot shrub called 'The Gift', she did some

The wheelbarrow of spent roses parked in front of freshly blooming *R. multiflora* indicates that her peak of bloom comes late in the season.

research. Karen concluded that my rose was most likely *Rosa multiflora* and 'The Gift' was probably a sport. When I looked up *R. multiflora* in one of my gardening books, the examples I saw were bright pink. Now I was thoroughly confused. My rose was the wrong color and had four possible names.

"Misnamed" roses are an infamous category of the genus *Rosa*. Since few roses begin with the letter *X*, 'Madame X' stands in as an alias in my alphabet and stimulates a discussion on misnomers.

Wiring *Rosa multiflora* hips on a metal hoop makes a fun wreath.

Disputes in the rose world are customary according to American author and rose lover Thomas Christopher. In his book, *In Search of Lost Roses*, he equates the confusion rose rustlers got into when their Old Rose discoveries started acquiring more than one name to the perspective of the first French rose nurseryman, Monsieur J. P. Vibert. In his catalog of 1830 Vibert writes, "It is the privilege of beautiful roses to have many names."

Christopher goes on to say: "In Vibert's opinion, a noble rose was like a nobleman; the more important he was, the more titles he should bear. Some of the roses Vibert grew had ten names, every one as good as another."

My puzzlement over 'Madame X's' name ended in the spring of 2000 when a visitor from Ithaca, New York, caught sight of her in my garden and burst out enthusiastically, "*Rosa multiflora!*"

Amazed, I said, "What? You know this rose?"

She said, "I'm very familiar with *Rosa multiflora*. It grows wild near my home."

Rosa multiflora is a famous species rose from Eastern Asia. Sometimes called 'The Bramble Rose', *R. multiflora* has numerous progeny. Cultivated forms of this climber have long been grown in Chinese gardens. At Eccleston Square in London, Susan and I saw a pink Multiflora blooming profusely high up into the branches of trees. A wild type similar to mine, known as 'Snow on a Visit' to the Chinese, was sent from Japan to France in 1862. It proved to be of great value both as stock on which to graft other varieties and as a parent. Her genes are included in Hybrid Musks,

For matching bouquets, I work on them at the same time. It was easy to insert the roses in an ample base of *R. multiflora*.

Ramblers, Modern Shrubs, Polyanthas, Floribundas, and Modern Climbers.

Once my fence was covered, *R. multiflora* kept spreading. During the growing season, I cut off invasive branches. I'm thankful that her suckers don't travel too far, but I dig up strays occasionally. The rose gets cut way back in the winter. I have to be careful, though; while pruning, I always seem to get captured by small, sickle-like, very sharp thorns on long, grabbing canes.

I started experimenting with bouquets like the one I saw at Filoli when my garden became well endowed with roses. With my husband regularly turning out terrific ceramic vessels and vases, inspiration quickly became reality. My kitchen and living room frequently succumbed to the litter and debris of an intense rose-arranging episode, and my family became used to wading through drifts of petals, twigs, and leaves.

One of the most joyful aspects to a creative life is receiving inspiration from other creative people. I treasure the occasions like the flower show that give me ideas and broaden my outlook. Added to the ever-present inspiration from family, friends, culture, nature, and gardens—the creative life knows no bounds.

That wonderful day at Filoli magnified and confirmed my rose dreams and provided my garden with a misnamed memento that fills in for my alphabet's *X*.

Opposite: *Rosa multiflora* and pink roses mimic the design on a porcelain cup.

A DISEASE CALLED RRD

From the Midwest to the East Coast in the 1930s, '40s, and '50s, *Rosa multiflora* was planted by the thousands. It was used for soil stabilization, hedging, erosion control, and land reclamation. This over-planting caused a disease called RRD to appear in roses with Multiflora genes. Many of the dense plantings have been ripped out, but the disease still persists. RRD is characterized by aberrant growth on a cane. Removing the entire cane, if caught in time, can save an affected rose. Last spring a cane on my 'Kathleen' had RRD. Since I removed the cane, there has been no further signs of disease.

YVES PIAGET

Fully open blooms of 'Yves Piaget' arranged in a handblown glass bowl

When I see 'Yves Piaget' in full bloom, I think of Francesca, the daughter of Robineve Cole, my dear friend and former business partner. Francesca was only three-years-old when she lifted the enormous deep pink rose out of a bud vase in our living room and buried her nose in the fragrant center petals. For at least thirty seconds, 'Yves Piaget' covered Francesca's face—I could only see her golden curls.

'Yves Piaget', named after the French watchmaker, was introduced in France in 1985. He is M. L. Meilland's attempt to produce the look of an Old Rose on a modern repeat-blooming shrub. 'Yves Piaget' amazes his admirers and is the winner of three European fragrance awards. A Hybrid Tea measuring three to four feet, the shrub form is stiff and upright, which hardly matters since he produces such knockout blooms.

The flowers are heavy on stems that are only medium in length. The bush in my garden is oddly short compared to others I have observed, but it has a nice, although modest, batch of blooms. I need to acquire two more shrubs so I can depend on having more flowers to cut. Up to now, I have mainly used 'Yves Piaget' in bud vases or floating arrangements.

FRANCESCA LIFTED THE ENORMOUS DEEP PINK ROSE OUT OF A BUD VASE AND BURIED HER NOSE IN THE FRAGRANT CENTER PETALS. FOR AT LEAST THIRTY SECONDS, 'YVES PIAGET' COVERED FRANCESCA'S FACE—I COULD ONLY SEE HER GOLDEN CURLS.

Francesca with 'Yves Piaget'

The flamboyantly ruffled petals of 'Yves Piaget'—like full-skirted evening gowns—remind me of my life as a fashion designer with Robineve.

Business partners are much like marital partners; for eight years, I saw Robineve more than I did my husband, Leroy. We shared the ups and downs of daily life in a bustling, wholesale fashion business. Together we were challenged by the whims of style and change to create five fashion collections a year. The evening wear we designed sold in specialty stores like Saks Fifth Avenue and over one hundred small, sophisticated boutiques across America.

Our business, Carolyn Parker Designs, specialized in original appliqué designs—luxurious cloth cutouts ranging from roses to starbursts—that we stitched on to fine fabrics. One holiday season, we embellished the quilted silk bodices of strapless gowns with birds and peonies. For a spring showing we appliquéd geometric shapes to sheer linen dresses. A winter collection featured jewel-toned phoenixes and Japanese symbol motifs strikingly arranged on magenta wool. To incorporate handmade roses in a holiday collection of 1940s-inspired silk organza and crepe de chine dance dresses, Robineve and I even learned the French art of silk rose making.

We relished our quarterly adventures in New York during the fashion market weeks. We spent the days showing our collection to buyers at our Seventh Avenue showroom and searching fabric houses for selections for the next season. In the evenings and on the weekend, we window-shopped

The beautiful lime green leaves behind 'Yves Piaget' is *R. roxburghii*, my favorite rose filler for arrangements.

Fifth Avenue and kept up with the latest fashions displayed in New York's fabulous stores. We also enjoyed perusing jewelry stores, floral shops, and museums. Late dinners, plays, and movies rounded out our expeditions. Once we were back in subur-

ban California, Robineve and I translated the latest trends into our own designs.

One day, to our astonishment, we concluded that we had had enough of the fashion world and discussed closing our business. A week later, we

'Yves Piaget', caught by the sprinkler and my camera, in a silver cup

began liquidating. We had no idea where our business paths would take us, but we were ready for a change and Robineve was about to get married.

For her wedding, Robineve wore a white organza and silk crepe gown that she had designed for our last collection. I fashioned a spray of white silk peonies and celadon velvet leaves for her hair. My garden supplied 'French Lace' roses for her bridal bouquet.

As the years passed, I delved deep into rose gardening and photography, and Robineve became an interior designer. Our experience with color, proportion, style, and fabrics translated easily to our new careers. The worldly jaunts and business experience were also invaluable.

My daughters were then in high school. Robineve had no children and longed for fulfillment as a mother. A loving friend told Robineve about a young, unwed, pregnant woman who was trying to find adoptive parents. With great joy, in July of 1994, Robineve and her husband, John, attended the birth of their beautiful, soon-to-be-adopted daughter, Francesca.

As Robineve learned how to mother her precious baby girl, I was putting the finishing touches on the manuscript for *The Poetry of Roses*. I had so much fun taking pictures of the two of them, designing birth announcements, and giving them a baby shower in the garden. I strung a clothesline across the 'Cécile Brünner' arch and hung it with tiny booties. An old-fashioned bassinet became the receptacle for dozens of garden roses and baby gifts, and Francesca delighted admiring guests while laying on a blanket on the grass.

Robineve and I treasure our long and deep association. We are amazed at the different paths we have taken in our love for beauty. It seems lifetimes ago that we were scrambling to come up with our latest fashion collection. At seven years old, Francesca helped me recreate my memory of her with 'Yves Piaget'. But this time while she held the rose to her nose, she said, "I think this rose smells too much!"

ZÉPHIRINE DROUHIN

'Zéphirine' and forget-me-nots in a McCoy vase

"What is your *Z*?" That was one of the first things people unfamiliar with the world of roses asked me when they found out I had created a rose alphabet. They couldn't imagine a rose name beginning with this challenging last letter.

I enjoyed rolling out the answer, "'Zéphirine Drouhin'."

Since 1868, her moniker has been the finale in rose indexes. Her name somehow endears itself to rose lovers. Some of us are more familiar with this lyrical name than we are with the rose it represents. Zyphyros, the Greek god of the West Wind, gave Greek, Latin, and Middle English the root word meaning a gentle breeze—*zephyr*. Someone in France made use of the word to coin a feminine name—Zéphirine.

A little-known hybridizer named Bizot christened his only rose creation 'Zéphirine Drouhin', after the wife of a distinguished French horticulturist. The dictionary says *zephyr* also means "something airy"—which uncannily describes Bizot's rose.

I purchased the rose two years ago hoping to grow, arrange, and photograph her for this chapter. I'll admit that at first I thought little of her modest flowers. When compared to a bloom like 'Yves Piaget' (page 176), 'Zéphirine's' dab of petals seemed so insignificant. And her color, well, to be honest I thought it was close to garish. I only grew her because I needed to complete my alphabet.

AT SISSINGHURST, SHE WAS TRAINED AS A LARGE MOUND OVER SIX FEET HIGH. HER LOOSE, AIRY FLOWERS HAD A CASUAL EXUBERANCE THAT MADE ME SMILE.

'Zéphirine Drouhin' at Sissinghurst Castle

In the spring, the shrub grew well, boasting lots of bronzy maroon new growth. She filled with buds, and I tried to figure out an angle for a good photograph of her in the garden. As she bloomed, my prejudice softened a little, but time ran out and my chance for a picture evaporated. Since Susan and I were about to leave for England, I thought, "Oh, I'll photograph 'Zéphirine' over there."

I made a note to remind myself to look for her as we toured gardens. But I didn't have to— 'Zéphirine Drouhin' was waiting for me!

Our first stop in England was Hever Castle. Susan wanted to see this thirteenth-century childhood home of Anne Boleyn, the infamous Queen of Henry VIII. We walked through an extensive walled garden of mostly modern roses. At the far end, in full bloom, there she was. 'Zéphirine' proudly grew ten feet up a sunny wall. She looked great, but I didn't have my camera with me! I hoped that I had not missed my chance to take a photo worthy of Z.

In the afternoon, we toured Sissinghurst. I had read so much about this famous garden created in the 1930s by Vita Sackville-West and her husband, Sir Harold Nicolson. As we entered the rose garden, there she was again! 'Zéphirine' cheerfully greeted us at the peak of bloom.

The esteem I had for my alphabet's Z grew immensely. We saw her often in England, and one day, 'Zéphirine' showed me her brilliance at two renowned gardens. At Sissinghurst, she was trained as a large mound over six feet high. Her loose, airy flowers had a casual exuberance that made me

'Zépherine' as she looks today, climbing our fence with the school in the background.

smile. I was delighted to get a good picture of her.

'Zéphirine Drouhin' is a Bourbon rose with an enchanting fragrance of Old Rose and citrus. Thornless branches make her an ideal rose for schoolyards, corners, and picket fences. Not a great rebloomer, she also has a tendency to mildew. I planted my shrub to ensure plenty of air circulation. So far, the mildew has been minimal. I now welcome everything about 'Zéphirine Drouhin', even her shocking-pink flowers.

In many of England's gardens, roses are honored for their place in history and allowed enough space to display their full character. Time and again, exhibits of this admiration were a revelation. Each garden had its own special collection. Thanks to Britain's considerably moist climate, gardeners have little need for irrigation systems. This allows unique possibilities for rose abundance, miraculous to my hot and dry California point of view.

Kiftsgate, a private estate, is home to the largest climbing rose in England. *Rosa filipes* 'Kiftsgate' cascades its white, five-petaled blooms sixty feet up through trees and down into the rose garden. You can find other similarly flowered species roses throughout Britain, growing to their maximum proportions.

The rose garden at Nyman's, an estate donated to the National Trust, is like an enchanted land curated by fairies. Specially constructed arches and pillars honor an astounding array of Rambling roses (see page 160). Their myriad blooms, nodding in the breeze, overlook Gallicas, Albas, Damasks, Centifolias, and Mosses. Each rose is grown not only to highlight her individuality but also to provide the components for a lush garden picture.

The elegance of Major Lawrence Johnston's famous rose borders at Hidcote, another National Trust property, took my breath away. Full-blooming, richly scented Gallicas, Damasks, and Mosses introduced themselves as I slowly strolled in a blissful reverie down a long, wide path. Pillars of sweet peas bloomed in matching colors next to many of the roses, amplifying the intoxicating perfume in the air.

At Kew Gardens in London, the world's largest plant repository and research institution, I found what might be the most impressive three hundred acres on the planet.

In the renowned Palm House, a Victorian vision in glass and steel, I saw an elegant bo tree like the one that legend says Buddha sat under during his enlightenment. The shiny, pure black trunk of an ebony tree was a few feet away from the bo tree. In pristine health, they mingled in the atmosphere of a tropical rain forest with thousands of other trees and plants. In the lacy, light-filled Water Lily

'Zépherine' in yellow hobnail glass

House, I was entranced by sacred lotus and a range of pastel-hued 'Nymphaea' water lilies growing between the three- and four-foot-wide leaves of 'Victoria' cruziana water lilies. Mesmerized in a captioned rose garden, I traced the history of garden roses from Gallicas to Hybrid Teas. I walked through an arboretum of majestic trees that came from all over the earth and sat on a bench watching ducks cavort and skeet on a lake as dragon and damselflies lit from leaf to leaf. As planes from every country flew overhead from nearby Heathrow Airport, I thought how perfect creation is. How beautiful are the people, animals, plants, and objects of the earth. At Kew Gardens, I felt a special oneness and unity with our world.

More than ever, in the aftermath of September 11, humanity is seeking to know and understand itself. While finishing up this chapter, I came to a passage in *The Graham Stuart Thomas Rose Book* that could have been written about human beings:

> *As we study and seek to appreciate all kinds*
> *of roses so does our appreciation become deeper,*
> *finding more and more delight in color, form,*
> *shape, scent, and all other characters that are*
> *spread upon us.*

'Rouletii' and Banksia Lutea inspired an alphabet. I had no idea who the other twenty-four roses would be. One thing was certain, I adored roses and knew that every rose, including 'Zéphirine Drouhin', comes into form bearing many gifts. I conclude with gratitude for the joy of discovering and sharing the bounty of roses from *A* to *Z*.

'Zéphirine' in white hobnail glass on a tablecloth my mother embroidered in the 1940s

ARRANGING ROSES

Above: Prepped and waiting to be placed in the arrangement on the opposite page **Opposite:** It's a special window of time in the spring garden when all of my alphabet's roses are in bloom.

When I first began arranging roses, I had insatiable curiosity about how to make fabulous presentations. For inspiration and reference, I compiled a fat binder of arrangement clippings from interior design magazines. I also never failed to undress a bouquet in my mind when I saw one. Flower arranging books rarely satisfied my wish to know how an arrangement was put together. I hope this section will ease the rose-arranging process for you and answer your questions.

Without a doubt, an empty, water-filled container waiting for roses can be intimidating, even for me. Don't worry—a little planning with an understanding of your options will ease tension and lead to wonderful bouquets and arrangements. Most of the bouquets in this book are simple to make. Once you get started, you'll find that the methods described are flexible and interchangeable.

All the arrangements, except for one, were made from garden roses. This doesn't mean you can't apply the following methods to florist roses. But let me give you a tip: Often the leaves aren't attractive on florist roses, so it's best to remove them. Unless you are using filler (see page 202), keep the stems short and the blooms close together.

Observation is always the key to learning. Look at and study my alphabet's bouquets, try and figure out how they're constructed, then come back here for how-tos and tips.

Before we discuss arranging options, you'll need to prep your rose stems.

PREPPING

Cutting and preparing your roses correctly will ensure your cut blooms last and your rosebush stays full.

Morning is the best time to harvest roses; by the heat of midday, their strength is weakened. To promote quicker reblooming on your rosebush, make your cuts on a slant with the highest point above a growth bud that has five or more leaflets. Make the cut away from the center of the bush so the next rose will grow outward.

I often stay right in the garden to prep my roses after I've cut them. For me, thorn removers are a must for prepping stems. One whisk down the stem removes thorns and unwanted leaves. Heavier stems, thickly studded with thorns, like those on 'Pristine' (see page 114), require clippers or a florist's knife.

How many of the leaves you remove from your stems is up to you. In flower arranging, there's a rule to strip leaves that will be submerged in water. This is especially important for clear glass vases, because the leaves are not only messy looking they foster bacteria and make the water dirty. I sometimes break this rule when using an opaque container. If the container is roomy and I have fewer stems than I need, I like to use the submerged leaves for support.

With your roses cut from the bush, you'll need to recut the rose stems under water before placing them in a vase. This allows the stem to quickly draw in moisture instead of an air bubble, resulting in a longer vase life. This also makes it possible to keep extra large and long canes alive in water. I use a glass of water if I'm at the sink and a flower bucket when I'm outside. Cut the stems at an angle so stems resting on the bottom of the vase will not block water uptake.

Finally, remove any unsightly outer rose petals. Called "guard petals," they are the first layer and are often mishapen and discolored.

Now, place your groomed roses in the hottest tap water; it perks them up. Surprisingly, this treatment doesn't make them open faster.

VASES

If you have a garden full of flowers, your shelves should be filled with containers to show them off. I'm always on the lookout for new containers. Like fashion accessories, I can never have enough vases, and their use is subject to my mood

Make your cuts at a slant above a growth bud to promote new blooms. (Red leaves illustrate new growth.)

Thorn removers illustrate their use on the freshly harvested 'Duet' stems. Use these on florist roses too.

Cut stems of garden and florist roses under water to avoid air bubbles that will block water uptake.

As you collect vases, keep in mind how they will hold stems.

grids as a last resort; they're awkward if you need to remove flowers for maintaining or re-doing the bouquet.

WATERING

Roses are heavy drinkers; a many-stemmed bouquet can remove inches of water in a single day. The water volume in large vases like cylinders and urns is small and can easily be taken up by the stems. Always check the water level and replace the water as needed. And be sure even the shortest stems in the arrangement are getting enough to drink.

If you need a bouquet to last in an always pre-

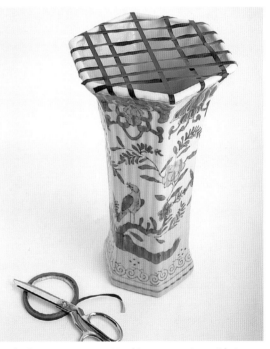

In the bouquet on page 52, this vase was too wide to keep the greens (which weren't quite long enough) in place. With a grid of florist tape over the top, I was able to anchor 'Snowmound' spiraea and hypericum branches so that I could comfortably insert the many luxurious stems of 'Graham Thomas'.

and style changes. So many vases and containers are affordable and some are free, such as jam and mayonnaise jars. Then there are the fabulous expensive beauties that you can dream about and save for.

It's especially helpful to begin observing the shapes and volumes of containers with an eye for how many blooms they require and how easily they'll accommodate arranging.

USING A TAPED GRID

Occasionally, you'll find the perfect vase that isn't quite perfect. If the vase is too deep and the neck too wide, you can try making a grid of florist tape over the mouth. You will then be able to anchor the greens and the rose stems. I use taped

sentable form, you must replace the water regularly. Dirty water promotes bacteria that robs energy from your roses. Removing water from large arrangements can be tricky; I go about it in three different ways. The first option: Lift out the arrangement and hold it while another person cleans the vase and refills it, or carefully lay the arrangement on a countertop while you refresh the water. Flushing is the second option. Simply place the arrangement, vase and all, in a sink and run water through it until the dirty water is replaced. Siphoning the water is the third option. To siphon, insert plastic tubing to the bottom of the vase, making sure the vase is higher than the container you are siphoning into. Suck once on the end of the tube and the water will immediately begin to drain.

Today I had to remove water from nine centerpieces that couldn't be removed from the tables they sat on. I placed a long siphon in the vase, which was a 6-inch glass cube, and ran the siphon into a bucket on the floor. The water ran down the tube like a charm.

ARRANGEMENT STYLES

After experimenting with my garden's rose bounty for a few years, I found that there are four basic ways to work with roses: floating, hand gathering, bunching, and inserting.

FLOATING

If you need a low arrangement or your rose stems are on the short side, floating or the look of floating comes in handy. Resting or lying are probably better words for this arrangement style, because the roses usually need to rest on the lip of the

Above: To siphon water from a vase, place a bucket below the vase so gravity will expedite the water flow. Make sure the end of the siphon touches the bottom of the vase so it removes all the water. **Opposite:** Here 'Yves Piaget' blooms float in a deep handblown glass bowl. The arrangement requires some finessing to keep the roses in place. Cut the center rose longer to form a nice mound.

container and lean against one another for support. Experiment with balancing roses in different low containers to see if you can get by without frogs and floral foam (see page 200).

USING WATER VIALS

Water vials come in various sizes and are handy for keeping roses fresh. You might decorate a potted tree or topiary with roses using water vials. When my rose stems aren't long enough for a big bouquet, I'll stick them in a water vial and prop them amongst other stems or wire them in place. Or try adding roses in vials to a pot of pretty ivy for a quick centerpiece. And it's nice to have a few water vials on hand in case you want to give a friend a special rose from your garden.

HAND GATHERING

Gathering prepared flower stems one at a time and arranging them in your hand constitutes a "handheld" or "hand-gathered" bouquet. The same bouquet with a wire or string wrapped around it is called "hand-tied." Use this method for small, medium, and even large arrangements. You are only limited by the amount your hand will hold. It's an intuitive, even intimate, process that brings you in close contact with the beauty of your roses—and it's quick and easy.

Gather and arrange your prepped blooms, one at a time, into your hand. Observe how one flower relates to the next and place it to its best advantage. When finished, hold your gathered blooms up to your container to gauge where to trim the stems. Trim longer rather than shorter, and place them in the con-

Small, medium, and even large bouquets are possible with hand gathering.

It's exhilarating to make a bouquet as large as the pink one in such a simple fashion.

The lower half of the three *Rugosa* canes are naturally free of leaves, insert easily and form a nice mound. I use gloves to avoid prickles.

I needed roses on long stems, but there weren't many roses in my garden at the time. I made do by making low cuts on the shrubs that had roses. The canes are rough and crooked but insert easily and don't show in the finished arrangement.

A variety of long-stemmed roses and pink and white Japanese anemones easily stay in place in the base of rose greens. Alphabet members 'Just Joey', 'Graham Thomas', and 'Pristine 'join *R. rugosa alba* in this arrangement. (For the final version see page 18.)

MAKING A LARGE ARRANGEMENT

Focal arrangements mean to grab the spotlight and often embellish a special occasion, so they're usually large. For the arrangement above, I wanted to use a spectacular container, but when the vase was full of water, it was too heavy to lift. Luckily, I found a narrow metal bucket that partially fit into the neck and was the right size to hold all the stems. I wired sheet moss to the exposed container.

FLORAL FOAM AND FROGS

The absorbent foam florists use makes almost any flower configuration possible. Floral foam comes in blocks that can be cut to shape and size with a kitchen knife. You can purchase molded shapes such as balls and hearts. The material must be soaked thoroughly before inserting prepared roses. I use floral foam for grand arrangements or when the other arranging methods won't work.

When I create an arrangement using a ball of floral foam, I find it's easiest to begin inserting the roses around the bottom of the ball and work up to the top. To maintain an arrangement of this type, spray the roses with water and renew moisture in the foam by spraying with a nozzle close to the material.

Not even three 'Graham Thomas' stems would fit into the narrow neck of this vase. A floral foam ball comes to the rescue. I removed the sepals before inserting the stems into the foam.

The short stems of 'Heritage' and 'Silver Sheen' pittosporum would scatter and pop out of this wide-mouthed container without a chunk of foam to anchor them.

Floral foam structure for the arrangement on page 188 after the roses were removed

A frog keeps the hydrangea leaves and 'Honor', 'White Masterpiece', 'Snowbird', and 'Evening Star' roses in place for a gorgeous centerpiece.

Floral foam has generally replaced frogs, but frogs are a great help when using a clear container. I also sometimes use six-inch diameter frogs when making a large arrangement that requires big bunches. A frog with sharp prongs will do wonders to keep tree branches in place.

A frog adhered to a bowl with floral clay forms a sturdy base to hold the stems.

GREENS IN ARRANGEMENTS

Greens provide structure and design to an arrangement. They offer support to rose stems and assistance to the arranger. My favorite greens to use for a bouquet are rose leaves. Many once-blooming Old Roses send out an abundance of magnificent new growth before and after their bloom. Rose leaves are often unique—interesting in shape and texture. Leaves I like are those of 'Common Moss', 'Golden Chersonese', 'Lady Banks', 'Mme Hardy', 'Quatre Saisons', *R. moyesii*, *R. multiflora*, *R. glauca*, *R. rugosa*, 'Schoener's Nutkana', *R. spinosissima*, and my favorite, 'The Chestnut Rose' (*R. roxburghii*).

Other good greens that harmonize well with roses are myrtle, 'Philadelphus', eucalyptus, Japanese maple, abelia, salal, spirea, deutzia, buckthorn, viburnum, boxwood, laurel, pittosporum, ferns, feverfew, catmint, lamb's ears, artemisia, pelargonium, ivy, honeysuckle, clematis, and solanum.

Be generous when filling a vase with greens. If you're creating a frontal arrangement and a branch bends to the right, place it on the right side of the vase. Try not to think too much—just do it. When you're finished, the base of greens often looks like a bouquet by itself. In many instances, the greens will barely be visible once the roses are inserted, however the structure they provide is critical to the ease of arranging. Once the greens are in place, you have the luxury and delight of placing roses that will stay put. Make sure your roses are dethorned so the thorns won't get caught on leaves and other stems as they go in.

In conclusion, keep your eyes open for inspiration; scrutinize the design work of others. Visit the storefronts and Web sites of high-end florists. Don't be afraid to start over if your arrangements look a bit jumbled. Experimenting and experience are your friends, and roses love to be harvested and arranged. Have fun!

Blooming *R. multiflora* provides a lavish base for white roses.

The arrangements of 'Elina' on pages 40-42 are created from a base of 'Philadelphus' (mock orange). Feverfew, long grass stems, a stem of euphorbia, a few stems of yarrow, and honeysuckle were then added along with numerous stems of 'Elina'.

ROSE GREENS

The unique quality of the leaves is evident in this display of rose branches. Middle top: unknown mini From top left: 'Rouletii', *R. roxburghii*, 'Cécile Brünner' From bottom left: *R. spinosissima*, 'Comon Moss', Rugosa

My favorite rose green, 'The Chestnut Rose' (*R. roxburghii*)

OTHER GREENS

Pelargonium

Variegated buckthorn

Myrtle

Sage-leaf artemisia

Abelia

Japanese maple

RESOURCES

SUPPLIES

Special materials mentioned in pages 188–203, such as rose dethorners, sheet moss, wire, floral tape, floral foam, water vials, and frogs, are valuable aids and are available at craft stores and florists.

ROSE NURSERIES

THE ANTIQUE ROSE EMPORIUM
A source for own-root, old garden and antique roses. They mail-order 2 gallon roses from October through the end of April. See the roses growing in their lively display gardens.
9300 Lueckmeyer Road, Brenham, TX 77833
Phone: 800-441-0002
http://antiqueroseemporium.com

DAVID AUSTIN ROSES
Order English Roses from the source!
www.davidaustinroses.com

GARDEN VALLEY RANCH
A rose ranch so beautiful that it is also an event center. The nursery sells rose bushes, and during the season, they sell cut roses to visitors and to the trade.
498 Pepper Road
Petaluma, CA 94952
Phone: 707-795-0919

HEIRLOOM ROSES
Located in Oregon's fertile Willamette Valley, they mail-order year round and have an especially good selection of cold-hardy roses.
24062 NE Riverside Drive
St. Paul, Oregon 97137
Phone: 503-538-1576
www.heirloomroses.com

JACKSON & PERKINS
Celebrating over 130 years of hybridizing and growing roses, Jackson & Perkins ships roses and other plants to more than three million customers each year.
1 Rose Lane
Medford, OR 97501
877-322-2300
www.jacksonandperkins.com

PETALUMA ROSE COMPANY
Specializes in easy care hybrids and old time favorites.
www.petrose.com

REGAN NURSERY
One of the largest mail-order suppliers of Grade #1 bare root roses in North America.
4268 Decoto Road
Fremont, CA 94555-3204
Phone: 510-797 3222
www.regannursery.com

ROSES OF YESTERDAY AND TODAY
This charming rose source was established by Francis E. Lester in the 1930s with help from Graham Stuart Thomas.
803 Browns Valley Road
Watsonville, CA 95076
Phone: 831-728-1901
www.rosesofyesterday.com

SEQUOIA NURSERY
Owner Ralph Moore is famous for hybridizing more than 300 miniature roses. Mr. Moore's rose 'Renae', a (non-mini) pale pink climber is one of my great favorites for disease resistance, beauty, and constant blooming.
2519 East Noble, Visalia, CA 93292
Phone: 559-732-0309
www.sequoianursery.biz/

VINTAGE GARDENS ANTIQUE ROSES
An own-root nursery growing the largest selection of roses offered by any source in North America. Their wonderful catalog (which I highly recommend) offers a descriptive compendium of nearly 3,000 roses and is available for $10.00. They have a fabulous Open Garden on Saturdays and Sundays in May.
2833 Old Gravenstein Hwy. So.,Sebastopol, California 95472
Phone: 707-829-2035
http://www.vintagegardens.com

ROSE SOCIETIES

AMERICAN ROSE SOCIETY
A national organization with over 20,000 members dedicated to the enjoyment, enhancement, and promotion of America's floral emblem. Go to their Web site to find your local chapter and information you might need for growing roses in your area. Membership includes *The American Rose* monthly magazine and many other benefits.
P.O. Box 30,000
8877 Jefferson Paige Rd.
Shreveport, LA 71119
Phone: 318-938-5402
www.ars.org/

THE HERITAGE ROSE FOUNDATION
A nonprofit organization established in 1986 was founded and developed to preserve and disseminate education and information about old garden roses and their origins and history.
P.O. Box 831414
Richardson, TX 75083
www.heritagerosefoundation.org

THE HERITAGE ROSES GROUP
Formed in 1975 by Miriam Wilkins, this is a fellowship of those who care about the Old Garden Roses, Species Roses, Old or Unusual Roses, especially those roses introduced into commerce prior to the year 1867. They host the famed Celebration of Old Roses each year in May, in El Cerrito, California. Dues include a charming newletter; southwest chapters also receive two issues of *Old Roser's Digest*.
www.thefragrantgarden.com/hrg.html

WORLD FEDERATION OF ROSE SOCIETIES
An association of the national rose societies of 36 countries with information about the rose around the world.
www.worldrose.org/

GARDENS

DESCANSO GARDENS
In this International Rosarium, significant collections of species, old garden roses, and modern roses are arranged in theme gardens.
1418 Descanso Drive
La Canada Flintridge, CA 91011
Phone: 818-949-4200

FILOLI
A grand Georgian mansion surrounded by a 654-acre estate garden, in the San Fransciso Bay area, represents the golden age of American gardens.

86 Canada Road
Woodside, CA 94062
Phone: 650-364-8300
www.filoli.org

THE HUNTINGTON ROSE GARDEN
The Rose Garden, consisting of approximately 1,200 cultivars, is arranged historically; in it, the story of the rose can be traced for more than a thousand years. Every two months they publish an e-newsletter "Subrosa" covering many interesting rose world subjects.
1151 Oxford Road
San Marino, CA 91108
Phone: 626-405-2100
www.huntington.org

FAVORITES

COMBINED ROSE LIST
Published annually since 1980, the *Combined Rose List* is the one international reference for rose sources. It contains essential information about rose varieties and mail-order nurseries in the United States, Canada, and many overseas countries. Information in this 264-page softcover book is provided for more than 14,500 different roses and more than 300 mail-order nurseries.
Peter Schneider
P.O. Box 677
Mantua, OH 44255
Phone: 330-296-2618
www.combinedroselist.com

ROGER'S ROSES
This Web site is a world encyclopedia of rose pictures and information based on the published (and unpublished) works of authors Roger Phillips and Martyn Rix, with a large contribution from Bill Grant. The site features over 5,800 pictures of roses!
http://www.rogersroses.com/

ROYAL BOTANIC GARDENS AT KEW
A vast horticultural treasury on three hundred acres located on the Thames River in London.
www.rbgkew.org.uk/

FLORALI
My friend Susan Donley, who I mention so often throughout the book, is a florist with a wonderful selection of vases and interesting containers.
2345 Boulevard Circle
Walnut Creek, CA 94595
Phone: 925-934-6877
www.florali.com

BIBLIOGRAPHY

Austin, David. *David Austin's English Roses*. Little, Brown, 1993.

Beales, Peter. *Classic Roses*. Holt, Rinehart and Winston,1985.

Brown, Jane. *Vita's Other World*. Penguin Books, 1987.

Bunyard, Edward A. *Old Garden Roses*. Country Life LTD., 1936.

Cameron, Julia. *The Artists Way*. Tarcher/Putman, 1992.

Cerwinske, Laura. *The Book of the Rose*. Thames and Hudson, 1992.

Christopher, Thomas. *In Search of Lost Roses*. Summit Books, 1989.

Cox, Jeff. *Landscape with Roses*. The Taunton Press, 2002.

Cloutman, Paul. *Royal Botanic Gardens Kew*. The Bath Press, 2001.

Crookston, Peter. "Gardens Illustrated." The Collectors, 2000.

Dean, Judy, and Lynne Storm, and Bev Vienna. *Field Report of Rose Characteristics*. Self published, 2002.

Fisher, John. *The Companion to Roses*. Salem House Publishers, 1987.

Fonteyn, Margot. *The Magic of Dance*. Alfred A. Knopf, New York, 1979.

Gibson, Michael. *The English Rose Garden*. Shire Publications, 2000.

Grimshaw, Dr. John. *The Gardener's Atlas*. Firefly, 1998.

Harkness, Jack. *Roses*. JM Dent & Sons LTD, 1978.

Hole, S. Reynolds. *A Book About Roses*. Edward Arnold, 1896.

Hobhouse, Penelope. *Color in Your Garden*. Little, Brown, 1996.

Jekyll, Gertrude. *Colour Schemes for the Flower Garden*. Antique Collector's Club, 1996.

Krasovskaya, Vera. *Nijinsky*. Schirmer Books, 1979.

Le Normand, M. A. *Historical and Secret Memoirs of the Empress Josephine*. Carey and Hart, 1852.

Lester, Francis E. *My Friend the Rose*. Mount Pleasant Press, 1942.

Lowery, Gregg. Vintage Gardens Catalogue.

Martin, Clair G. *100 Old Roses for the American Garden*. Workman, 1999.

McMahon, Christopher, and Timmy Gallagher. *The Gardens at Filoli*. Pomegranate, 1994.

Pavord, Anna. *Hidcote Manor Garden*. The National Trust, 1993.

Peck, Ann. "Roses Rosette: The Early Years." Heritage Roses Newsletter, 2001.

Phillips, Roger, and Leslie Land. *The 3000 Mile Garden*. Penguin Books, 1992.

Phillips, Roger, and Martyn Rix. *The Quest for the Rose*. Random House,1993.

———. *Roses*. Random House, 1988.

Pope, Nori and Sandra. *Colour by Design*. Conran Octopus, 1998.

Ray, Richard, and Michael MacCaskey. *Roses*. HPBooks, 1985.

Redell, Rayford. *The Rose Bible*. Harmony Books, 1994.

Scanniello, Stephen, and Tania Bayard. *Roses of America*. Henry Holt & Company, 1990.

Scarry, Elaine. *On Beauty*. Princeton University Press, 1999.

Scarman, John. *Gardening with Old Roses*. Harper Collins, 1996.

Shepherd, Roy E. *History of the Rose*. Macmillan, 1954.

Shoup, Mike. *In Search of the Forgotten Rose*. OGR & Shrub Gazette, 2001.

Spry, Constance. *Flower Decoration*. 1934. Reprint, Academy Chicago Publishers, 1993.

Svoboda, P., and J. Kaplicka. *Beautiful Roses*. Artria, 1965.

Thomas, Graham Stuart. *The Graham Stuart Thomas Rose Book*. Sagapress, 1994.

———. *An English Rose Garden*. Michael Joseph, 1991.

———. *A Garden of Roses*. Salem House, 1987.

———. The Manual of Shrub Roses. Sunningdale Nurseries, 1964.

Verrier, Suzanne. *Rosa Gallica*. Capability's Books, 1995.

Westrich, Josh. *Old Garden Roses and selected modern hybrids*. Thames and Hudson, 1971.

Winterrowd, Wayne. *Roses: A Celebration*. Farrar, Straus & Giroux, 2003.

Wiley, Patricia. Roses of Yesterday and Today catalogue. 1991 and 1992.

INDEX